Facilities Planning for School Library to Technology Centers,

Second Edition

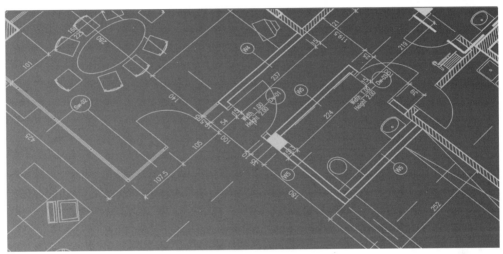

Steven M. Baule

Linworth
Books

Professional Development Resources for
K-12 Library Media and Technology Specialists

To My Wife and Children
Kathy, Sydney, & Sam Baule

Library of Congress Cataloging-in-Publication Data

Library of Congress Cataloging-in-Publication Data

Baule, Steven M., 1966-
  Facilities planning for school library media & technology centers / Steven M. Baule. -- 2nd ed.
      p. cm.
  Includes bibliographical references and index.
  ISBN 1-58683-294-8 (pbk.)
 1. School libraries--United States--Planning. 2. Instructional materials centers--United States--Planning.
3. Library buildings--United States--Design and construction. 4. Instructional materials centers--United
States--Design and construction. 5. School facilities--United States--Planning. 6. Educational technol-
ogy--United States--Planning. I. Title.
  Z675.S3B38 2007
  027.80973--dc22

                              2006034179

Published by Linworth Publishing, Inc.
480 East Wilson Bridge Road, Suite L
Worthington, Ohio 43085

Copyright © 2007 by Linworth Publishing, Inc.

ISBN: 1-58683-294-8

5 4 3 2 1

Permissions

Figure 2.4 Gambell Floor Plan reprinted with permission from Sharon A. Poor, Chief Communications
Officer, Fanning/Howey Associates, Inc.

Figure 2.5 Wilson Floor Plan reprinted with permission from Sharon A. Poor, Chief Communications
Officer, Fanning/Howey Associates, Inc.

Figure 3.17 New Trier High School Library Bubble Diagram reprinted with permission from Stephen J.
Cashman, Cashman Stahler Group, Lombard, Illinois.

Figure 3.18 New Trier High School Library Architectural Drawing reprinted with permission from
Stephen J. Cashman, Cashman Stahler Group, Lombard, Illinois.

Figure 3.6 Belinder Elementary Floor Plan reprinted with permission from David Reed, Vice President,
Gould Evans Associates, LC.

Figure 3.7 Belinder General reprinted with permission from David Reed, Vice President, Gould Evans
Associates, LC.

Figure 7.1 Photo of grand opening of the Shawnee Mission Northwest High School Library reprinted with
permission from Lee Anne Neal, Director of Communications, Shawnee Mission School District,
Shawnee Mission Kansas.

Table of Contents

Table of Figures iv

About the Author vi

Introduction vii

Chapter 1: Getting Started 1

    Flexibility. 2

    Expandability. 2

    Security 4

    Planning Team. 4

    Key Team Members. 5

    Library Advisory Board Members. 6

    Educational Support Staff 7

    Outside Experts 7

    Planning for a New School 7

    Choosing an Architect 7

    Technology Consultants 9

    After the Team Is Organized 9

    Politics 10

    Renovation. 10

    Work with the Architect 10

Chapter 2: First Steps 13

    Site Visits. 15

    Site Visit Questionnaires 15

    Needs Assessment 16

    Design Discussion 17

    Determining Spaces and Areas Needed to Support Services 17

    Traffic and Workflow. 18

    Additional Resources. 19

    Placing the Library Media Center and Technology Areas

        within the School 19

    Proximity to Technology 20

    Library Media Computer Labs 20

    Expansion Options. 23

Chapter 3: Specifying Needs. 25

    Entering the Library Media Center 25

    Security 26

           Display Space 26

           Community Access 26

    Open Space Library Media Centers 27

    Shelving the Collection 27

    Plan for the Desired Collection Size 28

    Distributing the Collection 29

Table of Contents *continued*

New Technologies 31
Aisle Width 32
Visibility for Supervision 32
Display Shelving 32
Closed Shelving. 33
Student Seating 34
Seating at Tables 35
Table Shapes 35
Table Space 36
A Note on Tables 36
Soft Seating 36
The Circulation or Service Desk 37
Microform Areas (*if they are still in the collection*) 40
Conference Rooms 40
Story Areas 41
Audio Visual Production Area. 41
       Traditional Graphics 41
       Electronic Graphics 42
Audio Visual or Other Equipment Storage 42
Computer Repair Spaces. 43
Open Storage Space. 43
Network and Server Spaces. 43
Computer Spaces. 44
Productivity Software Access 45
Library Media Workroom 46
Library Media Specialist Offices. 46
Library Media Staff Break Area 47
Archives. 47
Putting the Pieces Together 47
Fine Tuning the Design 50
Furniture 51
Chairs. 51
Colors. 52
Computer Furniture 52
Furniture Arrangement 54
Enduring Styles 54
Electrical and Data Networking Needs. 56
Wireless vs. Wired Networks 58
Cabling 58
Conditioned Power 59
Lighting 60
Natural Lighting 60
Lighting Placement 60
Lighting and the Security System 61

Table of Contents *continued*

Exit and Emergency Lighting 61
Acoustics and Noise Reduction. 62
Color and Design 62
Signage 63
Directional Signs 63
Location Identification 64
Collection Signage. 64

Chapter 4: *Computer Lab Spaces*. 65
Presentation Issues in a Computer Lab. 76
Computer Supervisory Systems 76
Setting Up a Mobile Laptop Lab. 77
Computer Furniture 79
Ergonomics 79
A Note on Language Labs. 80

Chapter 5: *Sample Media Center Layouts* 83

Chapter 6: *Creating Bids and Timelines* 93
RFP's or Bid Documents. 93
Bidding Wiring or Electrical Work 95
Pre-Bid Walkthrough 95
Contingency Funds 96
Timelines 96
Backward Planning 97
Sample Timeline 98

Chapter 7: *Wrapping Up* 99
Moving Out and Moving Back In 99
Packing Up the Media Center 100
Weed the Collection 100
Unpacking 101
The Necessary Communications 101
Summary 102
Bibliography 103
Library Facilities-Related Web Sites 105
Glossary. 106

Appendices 111
A; Questions to Be Answered During Site Visits 111
B: Library Media Center Programming Document 114
C: Sample Specifications Form for an Area of the Library Media Center 121
D: Computer Lab Programming Document 123
E: Issues to Be Addressed in Bid Specifications. 130
F: Sample Schedule of Values for Computer Equipment 132
G: Common Table and Workstation Sizes and Shapes 133

Index 134

Table of Figures

Chapter 1
Figure 1.1 Sample Team Compositions 5

Chapter 2
Figure 2.1 Sample Space Needs 17
Figure 2.2 Placement of the Library Media Center Within the School 21
Figure 2.3 Middle School Floor Plan 21
Figure 2.4 Gambell Floor Plan 22
Figure 2.5 Wilson Floor Plan 23

Chapter 3
Figure 3.1 Collection Size Guidelines 28
Figure 3.2 Shelving Guidelines 29
Figure 3.3 Shelf Analysis 31
Figure 3.4 Periodical Shelving 33
Figure 3.5 Extended Shelving 33
Figure 3.6 Belinder Plan 34
Figure 3.7 Belinder Actual Photo 35
Figure 3.8 Service Desk Functions 37
Figure 3.9 Work Surface Heights 38
Figure 3.10 Model Circulation Desk 39
Figure 3.11 Circulation Desk for a Small Library Media Center 39
Figure 3.12 Charge Desk Blueprint 40
Figure 3.13 Wall Mounted Rack 44
Figure 3.14 Standing Rack 44
Figure 3.15 Open Wiring Rack 44
Figure 3.16 Open Wiring Rack 44
Figure 3.17 Bubble Diagram 48
Figure 3.18 Architectural Drawing 48
Figure 3.19 Computer Reference Area 48
Figure 3.20 Traditional Floorplan 49
Figure 3.21 Isometric Drawing 49
Figure 3.22 Story Area of the Library Media Center 49
Figure 3.23 Types of Standard Chairs 52
Figure 3.24 Task Chair 52
Figure 3.25 Side Chair 52
Figure 3.26 Standard Four Legged Tables 53
Figure 3.27 Furniture Edges 53
Figure 3.28 Furniture Bid Specs 55
Figure 3.29 A Data Drop 58

Table of Figures continued

Chapter 4

Figure 4.1 Traditional Lab 66
Figure 4.2 Column Lab 67
Figure 4.3 Horseshoe Lab 68
Figure 4.4 Alternate Horseshoe Lab 69
Figure 4.5 Wall Lab 70
Figure 4.6 Alterante Wall Lab 71
Figure 4.7 Island Lab 72
Figure 4.8 "L" Lab 73
Figure 4.9 Tiered Layout 74
Figure 4.10 Tiered Lab 2 75
Figure 4.11 Laptop Cart 1 78
Figure 4.12 Laptop Cart 2 78
Figure 4.13 Laptop Cart 3 78
Figure 4.14 PC Mounted Below Table 80
Figure 4.15 Numbered Carrels 80
Figure 4.16 Language Carrels 81

Chapter 5

Figure 5.1 Elementary Library Media Center Layout #1 84
Figure 5.2 Elementary Library Media Center Layout #2 85
Figure 5.3 Elementary Library Media Center Layout #3 86
Figure 5.4 Middle School Library Media Center Layout #1 .87
Figure 5.5 Middle School Library Media Center Layout #2 .88
Figure 5.6 High School Library Media Center Layout #1 89
Figure 5.7 High School Library Media Center Layout #2 90
Figure 5.8 High School Library Media Center Layout #3 91
Figures 5.9 High School Library Media Center Layout #4 Level 1 92
Figures 5.9 High School Library Media Center Layout #4 Level 2 92

About the Author

Steven M. Baule, Ed.D., Ph.D., is the superintendent of schools for Community Unit School District 201 in Westmont, Illinois. He was previously assistant superintendent for information technology for the New Trier High School District in Winnetka, Illinois. His professional experience includes classroom teaching and working as a library media specialist, a technology director, and a high school principal. Dr. Baule has also taught graduate courses in education administration, library science and technology management at several midwestern universities. Dr. Baule holds doctorates in educational leadership and instructional technology from Northern Illinois University and Loyola University respectively. He also holds a master's degree in library science from the University of Iowa.

Introduction

If you have picked this book up it is probably because you are about to embark on some sort of facilities project or have been asked to join a planning team. Congratulations! The experience of designing a new facility can be an incredibly rewarding one! You have taken an important step by beginning to become informed about facilities design and the design process itself. The emotions that you may be experiencing probably run the gamut from *I am totally in over my head!* through *I am not worthy of a new space!* to *I so do not have time for this! How will I get the rest of my job done this year!*? Do not worry; in the end, you will be able to look back upon your facilities planning work with great satisfaction. What you help create will most likely stand the test of time and will still be serving students long after you retire.

This text is divided into several chapters. The first chapter speaks to putting together the planning team and ensuring you have proper stakeholder involvement from the start of the project. Chapter Two outlines the initial steps to take once the team is formed. The next chapters explain the needs assessment process for both library media centers and technology labs. Chapter Five provides sample library media center layouts. Chapter Six presents information about creating bid documents, specifications, and the timelines likely to be followed in any facilities project. Chapter Seven deals with the post planning process of actually moving into the new space.

The appendices include a number of potentially useful documents for the planning team. Sample programming documents to assist in the needs assessment process are provided along with questionnaires to use when making site visits. Criteria for bid specifications are also provided along with a sample computer bid that can be used as a template. A table of common furniture sizes and shapes is included to help with planning. The last section of the book includes a glossary, bibliography of additional resources, and an index.

Good luck in your planning efforts . . .

Getting Started

F inding out that one is going to be part of a facilities design project is often very exciting. Renovating an old school or building a new school are not projects entered into lightly. After the initial euphoria of being part of such an exciting project, the scope of what must be done can seem overwhelming. Much of today's educational literature is focused on meeting the educational challenges of the new century. However, because school buildings often last more than 50 years, facilities planners need to take even more possibilities into account and plan for a diverse future. If one thinks back to his own school experience, the scenario was most likely rectangular classrooms with the teacher at the front of the class. It was the same for most of our ancestors who were lucky enough to attend formal schooling. Libraries have changed very little in their layout. Books and patron seating have taken up the majority of the space in libraries for centuries. In the recent past, some of the space previously dedicated to books and tables has been replaced by computers and printers.

Three basic reasons exist for embarking on a facilities project in a library media center. The first is growth; the library media center has simply outgrown its present facility. The collection may have outgrown the shelving area available, or an increase in student enrollment may require additional class spaces within the library media center. The second reason is to add additional services or modernize facilities. These are renovation projects that address CD-ROM and OPAC access. Computer workspace for the staff needs to be added. Due to additional community access of the library media center, a new entrance may have to be built. The third reason for a facilities project involves constructing a media center in a new building. These are by far the largest and most complicated facilities projects. They also require the most forethought and planning. New school buildings built today will most likely still be in service in 30 or perhaps even 50 years in the future.

Questions abound when discussing the needs of future facilities. What will the curriculum look like? What will business and industry expect of graduates? Will books still be part of the collection (Some may not like this question, but it is nearly guaranteed to come up in discussions with architects, designers, or board members)? How many computers will an average classroom need? Will there be "average" classrooms? Will students bring in their own computers or will the school provide them? Copper, fiber, or wireless networking? Technology will most certainly continue to infuse itself into the educational process, but in what ways and where?

Flexibility will be a key to success for school facilities in the future. If today's educational literature is accurate, teachers and students will work in increasingly diverse and complex ways, as the teaching and learning process continues to adapt to better meet each learner's individual needs. Some of the probable issues affecting education in the near future appear in the box "Issues Concerning the Future of Education."

Flexibility

The flexibility of the space encompasses more than the simple ability to schedule multiple courses or subjects into a given area. Flexibility needs to be present in the walls, the furniture, the lighting, and the technology infrastructure.

Planning for curricular change and accommodating a wide variety of teaching styles is another key to successful modern facilities. Continual evolution of pedagogical methods, including cooperative learning and problem-based learning strategies, will make it difficult to determine what the average classroom will look like in 10 years. Accommodation for a variety of teacher-led and student-centered learning experiences is important. In addition, library media centers will accommodate larger groups of students as interdisciplinary instruction and team teaching become more widespread. These larger groups will be in addition to an increase in small group study space. All of these requirements will need to be met without a dramatic increase in the library media center's overall footprint.

Expandability

Expandability is another key to planning modern facilities. This is especially true with technology. The number of computers in schools, whether purchased by the schools or coming in with the students, will increase. When planning for technology, possibilities for future expansion are important within the classroom and the library media center. Placement of the library media center near an outside wall allows for the physical expansion of the library. Allowances should be made for adding future shelving ranges. In addition, the ability to expand is an important planning point for network and cabling infrastructures. Thinking in terms of expanding functions and services is also necessary. What are those services that a library media center may need to provide in five or 10 years that are not required today? Particularly, how can the school service community needs in the future

ISSUES CONCERNING THE FUTURE OF EDUCATION

Bigger Students – the average population continues to get bigger and not only due to obesity. Today's fifth graders do not fit well into desks from 1930.

Block Scheduling at the secondary level – if student free periods either disappear or become limited due to block schedules, student access to library resources must be facilitated outside of the traditional school day or through class visits.

Competition – from third party educational providers, voucher efforts, and home schooling.

Flexible Groupings – students need more access to support materials to enhance curricula that causes more student movement between courses during a term.

Green Schools – there is some desire to work towards more environmentally friendly buildings. These are known as "green schools."

Inclusion – requires more handicapped compliant furniture, the removal of many tiered spaces, and wider aisles between shelving.

Mobile Furniture – even science demonstration tables are being put on wheels as wireless allows for fewer tethers.

Multiculturalism – library collections should include a larger variety of materials showcasing a more world-wide view of the human experience.

Multiple Intelligences – requires a larger array of support materials with greater diversity of the range of items necessary to support a wider range of teaching methods.

No Child Left Behind (NCLB) – with the increased focus on accountability and standardized testing, any new building or renovation project will need to be able to address the issues raised by the legislation. Some states are also requiring tests to be administered via computer. Such online testing can significantly tax the computer resources in many schools.

1:1 Computing – if a school, district (or even state) is considering providing each student a laptop, space must be made available to repair laptops, allow for wireless access, and provide access to power for the laptops.

Online and Asynchronous Course Delivery – the library media center may become the classroom for some computer-based course delivery or the resource center for students working independently. The resources to create blogs and pod casts may need to be provided.

Security – concerns may finally be the death knell of open campus designs. Students may need to be able to be secured in rooms with locks to mitigate the impact of an intruder.

Team Teaching – the physical space of library media centers has to be flexible so large group instruction can be more easily facilitated.

Universal Pre-School – many elementary schools will need to provide additional spaces and resources for pre-school aged children.

Wireless Networking – requires significant study as to where to locate access points, what kind of security will be required, and how wireless users will access library resources, printers, scanners, or other peripherals.

that today are either not provided or are provided through other government agencies. How can the needs of community groups be met, and those populations generally not served by schools be welcomed into schools? These may include the development of adult education or parent and child education programs for low income or English as a second language programs. The future may bring more extended day tutoring or enrichment programs to schools. Mandatory or free state sponsored childcare programs may change the nature of the student body and require additional types of materials to be collected.

Security

Unfortunately, one other important aspect of modern facilities planning is planning for security. In today's world, an eye towards safeguarding our students cannot be overlooked. Providing increased access for the community requires that security be present outside of the traditional school hours. It should be a given that the design team will at some point review the design with the district's security director or police liaison officer. The library media center is often the focal point of the school building and in today's world, the planning team owes it to both students and staff to review the final design from a security perspective. Security is especially necessary as extended hours are becoming more common in media centers and schools are opening adult tutoring and No Child Left Behind (NCLB) mandated study sessions in library media centers.

Planning Team

Besides all of the concepts enumerated above, it is also possible that the facilities planning team has to deal with administrators, school boards, or possibly others who feel that the library media center could be eliminated in new or renovated schools. They may argue that technology allows all of the world's information to be provided via computer networks. In one recent issue of an educational journal, two articles presented opposite ends of the debate on the future of print libraries. One article clearly stated that Internet access and related online technologies could replace the need for a library media center within a new school. The second article specified that this increase in technology would require school library media centers to be increased in size. Even where the need for a library media center does not have to be argued, the space to provide services in traditional formats may have to be explained and defended. The amount of shelving for the print collection may well be a point of contention among various planners, possibly even splitting the library media staff itself.

At its best, educational facilities planning is an exciting and rewarding experience. It provides a chance to explore the philosophical and educational underpinnings of what a school or school district believes to be important. At its worst, such planning involves late night meetings and scrutinizing electrical blueprints to ensure that each classroom has the correct number of outlets to support the rest of the plan and that the electrical work will still be within budget. As a member of a facilities planning team, one will experience both extremes.

Key Team Members

The early involvement of a variety of key individuals is crucial to the success of any facilities project. As in the development of any other project team, participants should ensure that the team is as representative as possible. Leadership is a primary consideration when developing the design team. If the project is small, encompassing only a single department or area, the department chair or the area administrator should lead the team. If the project scope is larger, the administrator charged with facilities or physical plant responsibilities should lead the project. In an elementary school or smaller secondary school, the principal should be the team leader. In any case, involve an administrator in the process. The technology coordinator or the network administrator is the other key player who *must* be included on the team from the start.

Teachers and library media specialists who will be using the new spaces should be represented. As a general rule, have leaders include at least one "end user" for each non-"end user" on the team. Students, especially at the secondary level, are the other "end-users" to be included. Also, include clerical and office staff. Including custodial and maintenance workers is a good idea. These are the people who have to clean the spaces and fix what breaks, so they have a unique view into what does or does not work. Though the business manager may not be involved on the team, keep the administrator and the superintendent up to date with all of the team's progress.

Some districts choose to include one or two representative school board members on the team. The school board members are key in selling the design team's proposal to the other board members and the community. Additional community members may be added to the team as well, depending upon the nature of the community. In a large project, including several community members is wise if a bond referendum has to be passed in order to complete the project. Look to local university professors, staff from the regional library system, and administrators from other school districts to assist the team in the planning process. In several states, the state education agency provides resources to assist local schools with facilities planning. A number of consulting agencies and universities can also provide expertise in the design process.

Figure 1.1 Sample Team Compositions

Elementary Team	Middle School Team	High School Team
Principal	Principal	Principal or Assistant Principal
Library media specialist	Library Media Specialist	Library department chair
Library aide	Library aide	Library media specialist
Technology coordinator	Technology coordinator	Library aide
Classroom teachers	Classroom teachers	Technology coordinator
Specials (art, music, etc.) teacher	Specials (art, music, etc.) teacher	Classroom teachers (representing all academic areas)
Teacher aide	Teacher aide	Teacher aide
Student representatives	Student representatives	Student representatives
PTA representative	PTA representative	PTA representative
Public librarian	Public librarian	Public librarian

When assembling a facilities project team for a library media center, computer lab, or other technology center space, consider the following specific issues in determining the makeup of the planning team. As with any team, leadership is important. In order for the team to be successful, place team leadership in the hands of someone who has a proven record of leadership within the school or district. Put this responsibility in the hands of a library media specialist, a technology coordinator, a principal, or another responsible administrator. The important item is not the person's position but one's ability as a leader. In a small school, include all of the library media staff on the planning team. In large schools, library media staff members need to be included to the extent that all of the staff's viewpoints are represented. At the same time, having too many of the library media staff may drown out the other voices on the team.

Teacher selection for the planning team is critical. Select teachers who are members of the library media center. More important, they should be good student-centered teachers who are respected by their colleagues. If possible, also involve one or two well-respected teachers who are not library media center users. The planning process may allow them to bring forth the issues and roadblocks that cause them not to use their present library media center. In addition to regular classroom teachers, it would be valuable to include special education, art, music, and physical education teachers at the elementary and middle school levels. At the high school level, ensure representation for each of the departments or divisions by teaching staff.

Library Advisory Board Members

Many school library media programs are beginning to establish library advisory boards or committees. It seems only logical that some representative members of such a committee would want to serve on the planning team for a new library media center. Do not include this group to the exclusion of all others however. Such advisory committees are especially prevalent in larger schools or districts where such a committee may be looked upon as "library cheerleaders" and not as a cross section of the district's faculty. Respected faculty who are not necessarily tied directly to the library media program will often be able to bring much more political muscle to the table than faculty who are looked at as tied to the library media program. In school politics, it is nearly always more persuasive to have a point argued by someone with no apparent tie to the issue than those who would directly benefit.

In fact, one may want to include only a couple members of an existing advisory committee and then use the advisory committee as a resource to review the design team's work. Using the advisory committee in a review process will involve more people in the process and will provide a set of relatively informed critics who will not be too close to the design process itself. In fact, for renovation projects in existing schools, it makes sense to post the design documents in the library media center or the staff lounge for all to review throughout the process. Posting such documents allows for maximum staff input. Often those not immediately involved will provide additional perspectives that the design team did not consider.

Educational Support Staff

Also select educational support staff including library aides, teaching assistants, computer support personnel, and similar individuals who are important to the functioning of the school. These people are often overlooked when conducting facilities planning. However, they can offer unique insights as representatives on the planning team.

Parents, students, and other community members may be included on the planning team. The decision to include these groups must be determined based upon the culture of the community involved. Such involvement can truly enrich the planning process and provide a better end product. With younger students, using focus groups during the school day can be an effective way of gathering input. Students with more maturity can be included directly on the planning team if the culture of the school allows for it. In one middle school, a contest was held to redesign the media center as part of National Library Week activities. Each student was asked to provide a drawing or map supported by a paragraph or two of explanation. Several of the concepts presented later in this book were gathered directly from, or derived from, those student responses. Planning teams should try to hold such a contest prior to any renovation or design effort. It is really amazing what interesting perspectives students can provide to the design process.

Outside Experts

Outside experts can enrich the planning processes on a number of levels. These people can be included directly on the team at times, but often their involvement is through focus groups or responding to design drafts. Many times, other educational professionals, university professors, and even vendors will offer their time to serve as outside reviewers and to provide commentary. Local public and regional library staffs may be able to provide a wide variety of professional resources. A local parents' organization can assist in organizing community focus groups to provide input.

Planning for a New School

When one is charged with designing a new library media center in a school that has yet to be constructed, they may have a more difficult time gathering a planning team. However, the same guidelines outlined above should apply. Many districts are beginning to identify the principal of the new building prior to construction. If this is the case, the newly identified principal should be on the planning team. In some enlightened districts, the school library media specialist is also appointed ahead of time. If one cannot identify team members who will be going to the new school, try to bring in volunteers who represent the district's best practices and are respected members of the faculty and support staff.

Choosing an Architect

In addition to the other outside participation, choose an architect and possibly a design consultant. An architect must be able to take the ideas and identified needs of the planning team, and commit them to paper in the form of blueprints and specifications. In searching for an architect, turn to other schools and libraries to determine which architectural firms are being used in the local area and which specialize in school or library work.

Some important keys to selecting the right architect for the project include finding someone willing to design around the team's specific needs. Some architects may try to bring "cookie cutter" design solutions to the table. These are architects one should avoid working with. Look for an architect who understands the needs of technology, yet can appreciate the worthiness of the print collection. Architects who want to severely cut print collection shelving without first learning about the school's needs should be eliminated from consideration.

In some cases, the district may already have a retained architectural firm. If the firm does not have a great deal of library media center experience, look to one of two options; hire a secondary architectural firm to deal with specific library media center issues or enlist the aid of a library design consultant. One may be able to find a designer who also has experience working in retail or college bookstores. These designers can also help to bring the best aspects of retail marketing to the facility. For contact information regarding either architects or designers, look to their professional organization Web site. These can often refer people to local chapters or members. The Council of Educational Facilities Planners (<http://www.cefpl.com>) will be able to direct prospective clients to their members in a given area. Another option is to find design support on the Library Buildings Consultants List developed by Library Administration and Management Association (LAMA) available at <https://cs.ala.org/lbcl>.

In some cases, one may simply be saddled with an architect who really doesn't either think he needs advice or doesn't care. One significant problem in designing school library media centers is that it is often one of the few areas within a school where the architect can be creative. Classrooms have retained their rectangular shape for about 300 years in America. Though there is some movement to change that, most schools are going to be made up of rectangular classrooms so the architect often looks at the media center as an area to express his creativity. Examples surely exist where creative architects created spaces that were visually impressive but not practical. If in doubt of "pretty but impractical" library media centers, one can review the photos of any school design contest. In most design articles, fully half of the photos show library media centers. Many have obvious design flaws. A lack of lighting control is a common concern in such library media centers. Also beware of round or oval library media centers; they tend to have less usable space.

Having an architect who does not always listen is one of the reasons it is important that one develop an excellent relationship with the school's leadership. It is imperative that one work to ensure input is received and accommodated. The simple embodiment of the library media design team is a good first step. Although the administrator responsible for the building project may allow the architect to overlook the team's input, he is less likely to ignore a planning team made up of several key faculty members who are concerned about the architect's progress. If all else fails, this is a time to strongly advocate for the library media program as the library media center that is finally built will most likely have an impact for 50 or more years. However, like any other decision, weigh the pros and cons carefully before charging into a situation and getting yourself mired in school politics.

Technology Consultants

If the project requires extensive technology infrastructure work, it is important to retain a data cabling or network designer. Often, such data cabling consultants provide a much higher level of up-to-date expertise in designing and installing a network backbone. In a best-case scenario, this consultant can provide expertise on both the data cabling (low-voltage) and electrical (medium-voltage) designs. For such consulting firms in the local area, contact BISCI (<http://www.bisci.org>).

After the Team Is Organized

Once a team has been put together, leaders should ensure that they regularly communicate with the entire school. The school community should have the opportunity to comment on designs or possible layouts. Where possible, design drafts should be posted in areas where the faculty can be easily exposed to them and allowed to comment. Each time the design team is presented with design documents that show significant progress or a new direction in design, it makes sense to post those designs for all to see and comment upon. For example, post data networking blueprints in the mail room for all of the staff to review and comment upon for a couple of days before the design is finalized. Set aside time at faculty meetings or in some other formal setting to provide interactive dialogue regarding the work of the planning team.

Before an architectural firm or any other outside consultant is awarded a design project, the team should discuss and agree upon several issues. Possibly the most important item is the scope of the project. Ensure that all parties understand the scope of the project and any limitations that have been imposed by the administration or the school board. The team leader must establish a clear channel for decision-making. Nothing can be more frustrating for outside consultants than to answer to all parties. Everyone's opinions and ideas need to be considered, but someone will need to be the ultimate decision-maker in order for work to proceed. Clearly identify what is expected from each participant at the end of the design phase. The architect delivers construction documents and most likely the majority of bid documents. The data cabling consultants provide wiring diagrams, specifications, and possibly product samples. Delineate who will be responsible for the final furniture specifications, the architect or the interior designer.

Politics

Most facilities renovation projects occur because someone at the executive or board level has lobbied successfully for them. New building projects often occur for the reason above or simply due to enrollment increases that cannot be otherwise accommodated within existing school buildings. It is not uncommon for a new Board member on the facilities committee to switch priorities to ensure he sees a new track built or the football stadium bleachers renovated. I have experienced several locker room renovation projects going forward when other areas, including media centers, were a more dire need. However, it only took one board member to change the direction of scant resources. Find an advocate on the administrative team or the board of education in order to make the project a priority.

If the project is based on enrollment growth alone, it is a near certainty that there will be a desire to reduce costs to an absolute minimum. If enrollment is growing fast enough to require new schools, the budget is already tight. In this case, the changes or modifications the team may want should focus on flexibility and what future moneys may be able to be saved for a small immediate outlay. Be able to speak about flexibility, total cost of ownership, or the potential long-term investment in a particular design feature.

Renovation

In the case of renovation, the project may be part of a larger renovation plan and if the team designs into too large of a budget, it is a simple decision to cut the library media part of the renovation. It is often the case that a renovation project takes on a life of its own and "scope creep" is very common. What to the original planners was a simple project quickly becomes a chance for every stakeholder to make just one or two minor modifications. It is a minor miracle to bring a school renovation project in under budget, so be prepared to compromise on issues that are negotiable.

Work with the Architect

A common misstep on the part of the school media staff is to articulate strongly that the architect or the administration do not understand the role of the school library in the curriculum. Unless the architect is brand new and working as a single practitioner, there is a very slim chance that the library media staff has more school design experience than the architect. Do not try to throw around the weight of expertise that the architect may not care about. If the school administration does not understand the role of the school library media center, the design phase of a building project is unfortunately too late to begin the education process. In the best situations, the architect will be willing to come and view the current library media center or visit some existing centers with the team to review needs. Good thoughtful architects will spend enough time in the current space to understand how that space helps or hinders the work of the library media program. In new building projects, take the architect and the design team on a field trip or field trips to review other media centers and computer labs.

Be wary of library media centers that have won architectural design contests. Many striking architectural features like large glass walls and two stories are not suitable for learning to occur. Also, remember that one needs to work with the administration and architects. In the end, they will have the final say on what does or does not happen, so please advocate smartly. Once one has turned the architect or the business manager off, it will be very difficult to get a further hearing.

Chapter 2

First Steps

A number of steps are taken once the planning team has been gathered. This initial planning process can be broken down into three phases:

- brainstorming,
- visiting other library media centers and libraries, and
- needs assessment.

One of the best ways to start the planning process is to brainstorm what the facilities being designed should look like or include in "an ideal world."

When the team first gathers, have the leaders divide the team into small groups and ask them to take some time to design their ideal library media center. Each group then reports their ideas and concerns as if they were planning the center. This process generally results in two products: an excellent list of starting points to consider in the initial design phase, and a development of genuine excitement among the planning team for their mission.

When conducting the brainstorming session, provide each group with an outline of points to consider while developing their ideas. If the group has a strong background in library issues or facilities planning, such a list may not be necessary. When providing an outline to the team, consider four basic areas:

- the instructional program
- patron services
- library administration (including technical services)
- technology infrastructure.

Refer to the "Team Outline of Points to Consider" on the next page.

Team Outline of Points to Consider

I. Instructional Program
  A. Instructional settings needed
  B. Types of classes to be accommodated (size/needs)
  C. Presentation needs
  D. Individual work v. small group v. large group
  E. Special needs students
  F. Extended hours needs, tutoring programs (immediate or projected)
  G. Co-/Extra-curricular needs
  H. Faculty and staff instructional needs
  I. Community and parent instructional needs
  J. Needs for parent meetings and assembles in media center
  K. Potential linkages with public libraries

II. Patron Services
  A. Leisure reading resources
  B. Study areas
  C. Shelving
  D. Signage and display areas
  E. Access to technology resources (computers and AV equipment)

III. Library Administration
  A. Circulation
  B. Supervision
  C. Work areas/office areas
  D. Storage

IV. Technology Infrastructure
  A. Data cabling
  B. Wireless access points (even if not planned for Day 1)
  C. Electrical needs
  D. MDF/IDF spaces
  E. Media distribution/satellite spaces
  F. Technical staff work spaces
  G. Hardware needs
  H. Potential spaces for laptop storage or security

At the end of this phase, it is time to bring forward any other planning documents in existence. Such items would include regional accreditation agency reports, strategic planning documents, building or district technology plans, annual reports from the library media staff showing usage statistics and annual goals for the library, and if this is a renovation project, blueprints of the existing library media center. Synthesize all of this information into a preliminary needs inventory. Then identify the types of spaces needed to accommodate these functions and services. Use this inventory to help determine the areas to focus on during the next sub-phases.

Site Visits

In the second phase, the planning team organizes a number of site visits to similar schools to view their facilities. In the development of library media centers and technology facilities, have the team also visit corporate and academic sites, as well as public libraries. The trend in library design outside of schools is to create more friendly non-traditional spaces. Corporate and academic libraries are leading this trend.

Sending the entire team to all sites is not practical. Therefore, before any of the visits are conducted, the team should develop a list of questions to ask and specific functional areas to see on each visit. Some advocate videotaping the visits, but good still photos will most likely serve the team better in the design process. Where possible, planners can arrange visits during times when the facilities will be in use by students and try to arrange time to talk to the staff who use those facilities. If practical, after the visit, arrange for the visiting team to sit down for lunch or dinner and talk through what they saw while it is still fresh in their minds. After each visit, the information gathered should be shared with those who did not attend the tour.

Site Visit Questionnaires

The questions should be developed for these site visits that are reflective of the needs and desires outlined by the group during the earlier brainstorming. The questionnaires should attempt to elicit the knowledge and experiences of the library and technology staffs at the sites being visited. Design these questions to address all four of the basic areas required in the planning process: instructional programming, patron services, library administration, and technology infrastructure. Ensure that any specific items brought up by the needs inventory are addressed. Some sample questions are below. See Appendix A for a more comprehensive list of questions.

Use the following questions to help gauge how similar the site's programs are to those planned for the new facilities.

- What is the total student population? How many staff members?
- How is the library media center staffed?
- What are the library media center's hours?
- How many classes can use the library media center at a time?
- How do teachers sign up to use the library media center?
- What subject areas use the library the most?
- What is the size of the collection (print, non-print, periodical holdings)?
- What thought process went into determining what balance they foresee between print and non-print materials?
- What is the annual collection budget? Other budgets?
- How do students use the library media center outside of class time?
- What other programs or functions use the library media center space?

- Do the library staff have their own work areas or do they rotate among several?

  Use these questions to help determine the advantages and disadvantages of specific facilities.

- Is there a good field of vision and supervision throughout the media center?
- How is the student flow through the media center?
- How are entrances and exits controlled?
- Is there enough access to computers, the Internet, microforms?
- How is student seating arranged?
- Where are the closed stacks? Who goes to retrieve those materials?
- Is there "off the floor" office space for the library staff?
- What kind of displays area are used?
- Where does the staff showcase new materials?
- How is the lighting in the media center?
- What area(s) is used for direct instruction? What would the staff like to change about this area?
- What provisions have been made for network infrastructure? (MDF/IDFs)? Servers?
- What provisions have been made for wireless networking? (Access points? PoE capable switches?)
- How many computers do they foresee being used in any given area? Desktops, peripherals, laptops? Do they connect via cables or wireless access points?

  Furniture is another important area to address during site visits.

- Would you use this same type of furniture if you were renovating the media center again?
- Are there times when you have to move (or stack) the furniture for other programs?
- How does the computer furniture address cable management?
- How do you use the furniture to mold student use of areas?
- Is the staff furniture acceptable?
- If you have "soft seating" in the library, what do you like/dislike about it?
- What are the dimensions of shelving, the circulation desk?

Needs Assessment

The third phase brings the team back together to discuss what they saw in their visits, what items they liked, and what their hosts shared with them. The team starts to develop a list of areas and services to include within the facilities to be designed. The third phase is also an appropriate point to conduct a library needs survey for the entire staff. The development of a needs assessment will give the team the opportunity to gather focused input into what products and services the library media center should provide from all stakeholders. Appendices B and D provide sample programming documents or needs assessment instruments that can be used as templates for the development of school specific needs assessment surveys.

Design Discussion

Any survey should focus on resources and services library media center patrons would like to access. It is also important to determine what issues may be hindering teachers or students from using the media center. Ensure that any survey addresses all of the issues brought forth by the needs inventory.

Determining Spaces and Areas Needed to Support Services

After listing each of the areas or services desired, several facets need to be identified: the type and amount of space necessary for the function, the technology infrastructure required, and lighting issues. In addition, determine where each area's location is in relationship to other areas in the floor plan. For example, one may want reference shelving close to reference computers and both of those spaces close to the main entrance. One would probably want a quiet study area as remote as possible from the entrance. When new facilities are being planned within the scope of a new building, identify space needs in relation to a standard classroom. This allows the architect to easily manipulate the design. In renovation projects, identifying space in relation to classroom size is less important as the overall footprint will most likely not change. In order for the architect to proceed, the team must identify what areas need to be near one another and which need distance between them. The end product of such a discussion may look like the chart below.

Figure 2.1 Table 2

Area/Services	Space Required	Technology Infrastructure	Lighting Needs	Co-Location With
Circulation Desk ■ Check out of materials ■ Check in of materials ■ Answer general informational questions ■ Provide supervision of student seating areas	.5 classroom	Data, voice, fax, electrical	No glare	Entrance
General Shelving ■ Hold print and non-print collection	3 classrooms			
Reference Shelving ■ Hold general reference collection	.5 classroom	Wireless access?		Need reference computers
Reference & Catalog Computers ■ Provide online reference services & access to search the library holdings	.75 classroom	Data, electrical	No glare	Near reference shelving
Class Seating ■ Allow for three classes to use the library media center at once ■ Allow for drop in student access ■ Allow for students to bring in personal laptops	3 classrooms	Electrical, wireless access	Natural light	

Figure 2.1 continued

AV Storage ■ Provide AV equipment to teachers ■ Support teacher and student presentations ■ General equipment repair ■ Storage of extra bulbs, cords, etc.	1 classroom	Data, voice, electrical	Full lighting	Near circulation desk
Closed Storage ■ Store back issues of magazines, CDs, DVDs, videos, class sets, etc.	.75 classroom		Variable lighting	Away from circulation desk and reference area
Story Area ■ Large group instruction ■ TV or video presentations	1 classroom	Data, electrical	Natural light, no glare	
Library Workroom ■ Process new materials ■ Administer the library media center	1 classroom	Data, electrical, voice	No glare	Near circulation desk
Student Production Area ■ Support student multimedia development ■ Suport student productivity	.75 classroom	Data, electrical, table space for work	Natural light, no glare	
Teacher Production Area ■ Support teacher multimedia development	.5 classroom	Data, electrical, voice	Natural light, no glare	Near professional library

Traffic and Workflow

In some cases, the planning team may not see location needs as readily apparent. In these cases, a traffic and workflow study can serve to confirm earlier decisions. A traffic and workflow will help the team determine the present high traffic areas and which functions need to be near each other due to staff assignments or requests made by users of the center. Usage can be determined in several ways. At the most basic point, the planning team can ask the library media center staff to keep track of how many interactions they have with people using the center. In a small library media center, this may be accomplished by placing tally sheets at each of the areas in the media center for the staff to use. In larger libraries, each staff member could also be asked to chart their flow through the library media center and designate what tasks they are completing at those times. In addition, student seat counts could be taken at standard times throughout the day to see how the student population uses the library. In a more sophisticated form, videotaping the media center traffic areas during high traffic times can provide useful data. Such traffic diagrams show how the students flow into the media center and the areas they tend to go to first. In addition, the flow pattern helps to highlight any obstacles to good traffic flow. Whatever the method is used for determining traffic flow, this information is important in planning both the overall layout of the media center and the design of specific areas later in the planning process.

At this point, the design team should be in the position to hand the above chart to the architect for preliminary design development. The architect should have a firm understanding of materials and services provided by each of the areas identified in the chart. If there are any special needs in a given area, set them forth at this time. The first phase of the planning process is complete.

Additional Resources

1. Information about the Council of Educational Facilities Planners can be obtained from their Web site at <www.cefpi.com> or by writing CEFPI, 8697 E. Via de Ventura, Suite 311, Scottsdale, AZ, 85258-3347.
2. Library Buildings Consultants List from Library Administration and Management Association is available at <https://cs.ala.org/lbcl>. This list has a public library focus but can provide contacts useful to school library media specialists as well.
3. Information about BICSI and the Registered Communications Distribution Designer (RCDD) certification program can be obtained from BICSI at <www.bicsi.org> or by writing to BICSI Headquarters, 8610 Hidden River Parkway, Tampa, FL, 336397.
4. For more information on developing a good relationship with the architect, see Haggans, M. (1998). 14 ways to get better performance from your architect, *School Planning and Management*, 37 (3), 24-27.

If this is a renovation project, ensure that the facilities planning team has its initial meeting in the present library media center. When necessary, provide time at the beginning of the first meeting for the team to get an in-depth tour of the library media center. If this is a new facilities project, have the team meet in a school library media center of the same type of building as the new facility will be.

Placing the Library Media Center and Technology Areas within the School

Another key concern is where will the library media center and computer spaces be located within the larger footprint of the school. This is an issue in any new construction project and potentially an issue in a large-scale renovation as well. Many library publications state that the library media center should be the hub of the school. The library media program can tie together and further support the curriculum of a school. The library media program should be the figurative hub of the school, but it is not necessary that the media center be the literal hub of the school.

In cases where the community will use the library media center outside of school hours, the library media center needs direct access to the outside. As many library media specialists are trying to provide extended hours for their traditional patrons, direct access becomes important. At the same time, do not place the library media center at the end of a corridor or far from the main academic sections of the school. Whenever possible, locate the library media center on the ground floor of the school. In schools that are arranged with a central core and several wings, place the library media center at the end of the central core to allow easy access to the outside while retaining its central position within the school.

Proximity to Technology

When developing larger schools, consider the issue of whether or not to consolidate technology facilities. The experts have not reached agreement on this issue. In many cases, schools are trying to eliminate all computer labs by placing computers in each classroom. However, as long as the curriculum includes the direct instruction of computer skills, high-end computers for computer assisted drafting (CAD) and graphic arts, and out of class computer time for students, computer labs retain a significant place in our schools. Once the decision is made to have computer labs, determine where they should be located. In small schools where a single lab serves the school's needs, place the computer lab near the library media center. This will facilitate student research during computer-based assignments, access to online resources, and allows for the supervision of both facilities when they are a part of a technology-rich library media program.

In large schools, the best practice is to distribute computer labs throughout the building and allow departments or teams to feel they have partial ownership of the facilities. When teachers can take their students into a lab without a long walk through half the school, they are more likely to use the lab. In addition, when they have a single lab supervisor to deal with, they feel more comfortable using the lab. It is also easier to place subject-specific software in distributed labs, so that it can be easily accessed by the most common users without requiring additional copies of the software or taking up hard drive space to place the software on all of the machines in a central lab. One might say that there is no need to put all of the software on all of the machines in a central lab, but then there is a loss of the flexibility of centralizing computers in a mega-lab. Labs often expand over time, and a centralized lab will at some point run out of room for expansion. Thus, some labs have to be distributed throughout the building anyway. The only real advantage to centralizing lab space is to reduce the number of staff needed for supervision. However, less supervision with the same number of users also decreases the amount of assistance available for the students. It makes a great deal of sense to decentralize computer labs so each area of the building has access to its own lab.

Library Media Computer Labs

At least one lab available for student drop-in work should be included within the library media center, or adjacent to the media center. Drop in labs facilitate student access to both library materials and the necessary technologies to complete technology-based assignments.

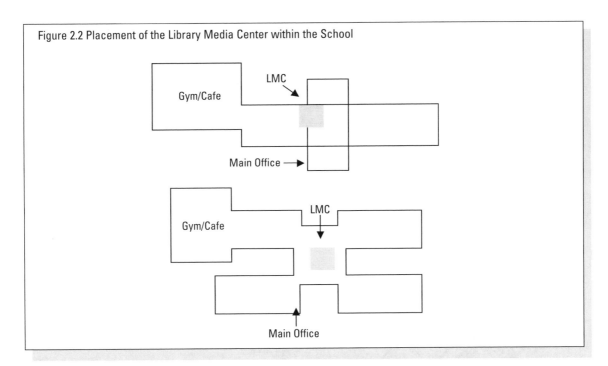

Figure 2.2 Placement of the Library Media Center within the School

Figure 2.3 shows a middle school design where the media center is truly at the core of the school. This placement allows the students and classroom teachers to have easy access to the media center from anywhere in the academic portion of the building. However, the design has the drawback of allowing for easy assess to the media center without allowing patrons access to other areas of the school.

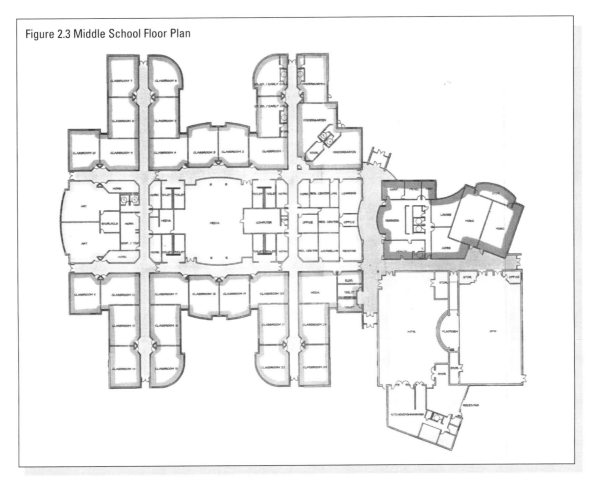

Figure 2.3 Middle School Floor Plan

The layout of the Gambell School in Gambell, Alaska is shown in Figure 2.4. This small school layout allows for easy access to the library media center from outside of the building for community use. The Gambell design is able to retain the library media center at the center of the school's academic space. The layout of Wilson Middle School in Muncie, Indiana, is shown in Figure 2.5. The Wilson design maintains the library media center at the core of the academic section of the building, but requires that after hours access will have to enter through the regular student entrance.

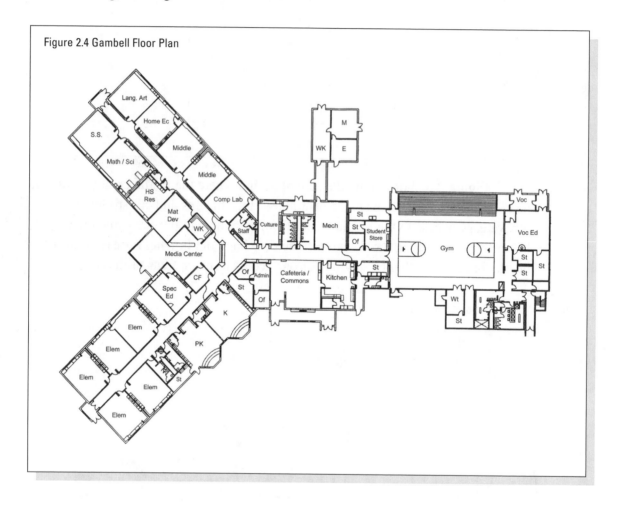

Figure 2.4 Gambell Floor Plan

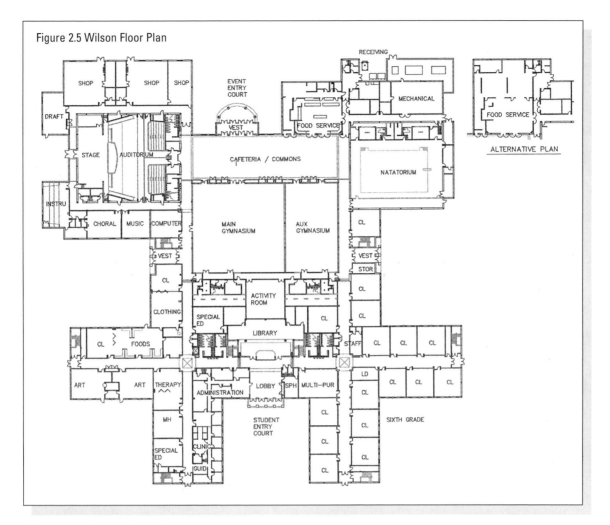

Figure 2.5 Wilson Floor Plan

Expansion Options

Another possible concern during placement is the ability for long-term expansion of the media center. If at least one of the media center's walls is facing green space or a courtyard, there is a greater possibility for future expansion

There are other concerns to address when placing the library media center within a new building. Where possible, if the building is to contain only a single computer lab, position the library media center adjacent to the lab. Reserve space for the building's network servers near the center so that problems with equipment do not require long travel for a response. This is especially important in small schools where there is no dedicated technical support within the building. In such cases, the library media staff ends up with the responsibility of responding to technology problems.

At this point, the design team should have a good understanding of what functionality the new library media center needs to include. The needs assessment surveys should have provided information from all stakeholders. The size of the media center and computer labs should have been determined and their placements within the school identified. The design team should now be ready to work with the architect to complete specifications for the new facility and its related furniture and technology needs.

Chapter 3

Specifying Needs

In the first phases of the facilities design process, the design team determined the overall programmatic functions desired by the school and the general areas to support these functions. For instance, if the design team has identified a need to circulate instructional materials, there must also be a circulation desk to check materials in and out, and shelving space to hold those materials between checkouts. In the next phase, the team must move forward from simply identifying the areas to developing specifications for constructing the areas, structures, and furniture necessary to support these functions and services.

Entering the Library Media Center

One of the first areas to examine is the entrance. It is surely one of the first areas patrons will experience. In schools, student control is always an important concern; the library media center is not any different. A number of items must be addressed in the design of the entrance. There should be only one entrance to the media center. A single entrance makes the supervision and security of materials easier and keeps students from using the media center as a hallway to get to other areas of the building. Another disadvantage in multi-entrance media centers is the high school "promenade" effect. Students stroll through one entrance, check out who else is in the media center, and then exit at the other end. Strollers can be extremely distracting to students trying to study, in addition to causing student management problems.

The entrance will need approximately 500 to 600 square feet if separate entrance and exit doors will be used. This space can be reduced in smaller elementary schools, but depending on the number of classes entering and exiting the library media center at one time, whether classes will line up in the library media center or the hallway, and the amount of display space desired. Remember that the entrance makes the first impression on patrons. It is important for the entrance to present an approachable and inviting appearance to visitors. Be sure that the entrance the team designs accomplishes both; first impressions are important.

Security is another important item to consider when designing the entrance. Most secondary media centers require some type of material security system at each entrance or exit to stop items that have not been checked out from leaving the center. When placing security systems, remember that some types of these systems are affected by the magnetic fields created by computers, photocopiers, and some types of lighting ballasts. Metal wall studs can even impact such systems. It is important to place the security system where an adult has easy access to stop a student who sets off the system alarm.

Display Space is desirable at the entrance to the media center. Divide this display space into two sections, permanent information, which includes information such as hours, a "no food or drink" sign, and similar materials. Use the other display space to announce new materials, Web sites of interest, or special activities. The media center staff may also want to include a book drop for returning materials after hours. In many cases, a fair amount of display space can be created by using an entrance with two doors separated by a center column that can be used as display space. A glass display case can be used to separate the entrance and the exit routes. Such a display case is an excellent place to display new titles, artifacts, or student projects.

Although dated, the 1988 version of *Information Power* remains one of the best sources for school library media design. Newer versions of *Information Power* have not addressed facilities issues. The 1988 version of *Information Power* suggested that the entrance be located near the circulation area, the workroom, and the reserve areas. Locating these areas together allows easy access to the circulation desk. As electronic resources have almost totally supplanted microform materials in school library media centers, computer resources in the form of ready reference computers should be accessible from the circulation area.

Community Access: If the possibility of providing community access during non-school hours exists, create a second entrance that leads directly to the most commonly used parking area. This entrance can be designed to sound an alarm when opened during the day, but ensure the alarm can be turned off to provide direct outside access at other times. Another possibility is to place the regular entrance to the media center near the school's main entrance, so evening visitors can enter the media center without having access to large portions of the building.

Providing direct access to the school through the library media center during the school day may seem like a good idea, but such access will cause the library media staff to become greeters for visitors. In today's security conscious environment, the school's office should be responsible for determining which visitors can enter the school. This should not become a task for the library media staff. If the library is to be opened to the community outside of regular school hours without opening the rest of the school, direct access to restrooms is vital.

Open Space Library Media Centers

Some library media centers in the late 1960s and early 1970s were designed as "open spaces." This design model is unfortunately again becoming popular. In these schools, the library media center is located in what amounts to an oversized corridor. The concept behind this design is that students can easily leave any classroom and enter directly into the media center to use the resources and services there. In some schools, this type of library media center is outlined with half walls or single-sided shelving to limit student access to defined entrances and exits. In some newer middle schools, this concept has a great deal of appeal as the library is then located between the various team pods and serves as a central focus point for students. In some schools, large group areas can also be co-located in this area to form a spacious atrium-type area for the school.

When planning, the planning team needs to consider the positives of an open library media center with some of the potential pitfalls of such a space. Hallway noise, especially in schools with staggered lunch schedules or passing periods, will interrupt those students working in the library media center. Security can be a significant issue in a media center without defined entrances or exits. Supervision can be difficult in a larger school where a student could disappear into a crowd by leaving the library media center in nearly any direction.

Shelving the Collection

The most important and largest single area within the media center is general shelving, "the stacks." The print collection will likely not shrink away to nothing because of increases in technology. However, in some school library media centers, this may happen because of a dwindling budget. In the foreseeable future, books will be a core part of the school library media center. Housing them is an important design issue. First, determine how many volumes the library media center collection must hold. Ensure that the planning team looks at any demographic data that has been prepared for the following decade or so. Do not base enrollment predictions on what size student body is being planned for (e.g., "we are building a 500-student elementary school"). Plan on what demographers say is the likely apex of enrollment (e.g., 650 students in 2008). It is easy to add additional classrooms or even mobile classrooms in the future. Expanding a library media center in the center of a school is much more difficult. In addition, school districts experiencing enrollment growth do not always have funds for areas perceived by some as "extras" like the library media center.

Determining the Size of Your Library Media Center

- The easiest way to determine the number of volumes required for the library media center collection is to multiply the number of students by the number of titles that the school would like to hold per student enrolled.
- Some states have established minimum or recommended numbers per student. Check with the state association or regional accrediting agency for recommendations.

The multiplier used can be determined in a number of ways. Several states and the regional accreditation associations have developed their own guidelines for library media programs. These are helpful numbers to use when one has to justify those numbers later. These requirements or guidelines are often influential with school boards and administrations. In many cases, one can determine a multiplier by looking at the existing collections within the school or district. In some cases, a state association or an accrediting body may have suggested a collection size for the school or another local school. The numbers in Figure 3.1 can also be used to help determine a multiplier.

Figure 3.1 Collection Size Guidelines

School Type	Student Enrollment	Multiplier	Collection Size
Elementary (K-5)	250	24 (books per student)	6,000
Middle School (6-8)	900	15 (books per student)	14,000
High School (9-12)	2,000	12 (books per student)	24,000

In a perfect world, the multiplier is adjusted upwards if the new media center will be serving a smaller population. Larger schools can also use a lower multiplier, as their students will still have access to a larger overall collection. A building of 150 high school students will not be able to support the curriculum with only 12 books per student. Likewise, an elementary school of 500 may not need 24 books per student to support their program.

The extent and depth of the curriculum is also important to consider. If a high school of 750 students offers only 50 to 60 individual courses, they will not need nearly the breadth of coverage a similar school with 120 individual course offerings. However, the school with limited curriculum may need more multiple copies of some titles. The collection size can also be affected by the standardization of a school's curriculum. If the school has a fairly tight curriculum, but each teacher sometimes teaches units in different orders or at different paces, then a smaller collection may be possible. In some cases, where the curriculum is tight across and all teachers maintain a similar pace, the collection needs multiple copies of many materials. Where the curriculum is more flexible, the collection should be more diverse to support individual teacher needs. Flexible curricula most likely require a larger and more broad-based collection.

Plan for the Desired Collection Size

After determining the collection size, the team can decide upon the amount of shelving necessary for the collection. Even if the team expects the collection to never grow by even one more item, plan to provide shelving for 120 percent of the preferred collection size. The 120 percent guideline allows for some room at the end of each shelf so that the books do not have to be packed too tightly when shelved. If the collection includes picture books, include shelving or bins for 200 percent of the picture book collection. Because the patrons who use picture books often want to look through the books at the shelves and generally have limited dexterity, consider picture book shelves or bins filled when only half their length is used.

Figure 3.2 Shelving Guidelines

Type of Collection	Multiplier	Collection Size
Elementary School Books	20	3 shelves high
Middle School Books	12	3-5 shelves high
High School Books	10	5 shelves high
Secondary reference books	8	3 shelves high
Periodical Shelving (Display)	1 title	3 shelves high (elementary) 3 shelves high (secondary)
Periodical Shelving (Unbound Storage)	50 (journal thickness) 100 (magazine thickness)	5 shelves high
Video/Audio Books	10	5 shelves high
CDs/CD-ROMs, DVDs	24	5 shelves high

Therefore, a high school collection of 20,000 volumes will need 2,000 linear feet of shelving or 4,000 feet of shelving units five shelves high. Since rarely will a school media center have all the shelving running continuously, it is important to determine how many volumes and how much shelving is needed for each section.

Distributing the Collection

Now that the collection size has been determined, decide how the collection will be distributed. Distribution is important because the collection is nearly always divided into sections, and it is best if classification ranges are not split between areas. For instance, one would not want the fiction section to be almost completely shelved in one area, and then have the end of the section across the room. Students would have a difficult time locating those items shelved in the second section. In most cases, the distribution of an existing collection can be easily determined if the collection has an automated catalog. Totals can be obtained from an automated catalog for each section based upon the call numbers.

In non-automated library media centers, estimate distribution by counting the number of shelves devoted to each call number range. Alternately, the catalog cards or an old-fashioned shelf list can be measured. Determine how many titles are in an inch of catalog cards and then mark the beginning and end of each call number range. Measure those ranges and estimate the number of items in each range using the estimated number of books per foot from the table above. If the team feels the estimated volumes per foot are not correct for the collection, complete a shelf count of 20 random shelves in the current library media center, and then divide the total number of volumes counted by 20 to determine the number of books per shelf. Then divide that number by the length of the shelf in feet to determine a local estimate of volumes per foot. In most libraries, this should be done separately for nonfiction, fiction, picture books, and the reference collection. See the example below:

- Count of five reference shelves: 84 volumes
- Shelving length: 36 inches
- Feet of shelving: 150 inches / 12 inches = 12.5 feet
- Average volumes per foot: 6.72 rounded up to 7 volumes per foot

If the team plans to allow for extra shelving at the end of rows for users to place books that they decide they do not want to check out, one will have to add that to the total amount of linear shelving needed. In many libraries, additional shelving is included in a slightly different color as a place for users to return items so that the users do not try to reshelve items. In cases where space is limited, a single shelf could be used in place of an entire tier of shelving. If this plan is used, the "reshelving shelf" should be placed in the middle of the shelving columns. Such shelving is not necessary with low sections of shelving. With low shelving, returned titles may be placed on the top of the shelves. If the media center has extensive special collections, non-print collections, periodical collections, microfilm shelving, or a large amount of reference indexes, averages for those collections should be developed separately.

When determining the amount of shelving necessary for future collections, the following observations have some merit. A common rule of thumb is that a new library media center should have shelves that are only two-thirds full to support growth, so modify calculations to accommodate the additional shelving if necessary. That is probably a good rule to follow if the media center is serving a new school that is being built to be further expanded in the future. It is common to build schools today in high growth areas so that additional wings can be added for future classroom growth. One of the problems with that line of thinking is that the core spaces including the library media center are rarely configured to expand as well, and they become quickly overcrowded when a building goes from 12 classrooms to 18 or 24 classrooms.

However, if the building project is not a new school in a fast growing area, that additional shelving is probably a waste of space and money. Print collections are not regularly growing today. That is due to two factors: the reduction of library budgets and purchasing power and the increased use of online and other electronic resources.

The print reference collection, though it will continue, will likely shrink in the near future. Encyclopedias and other general reference books are quickly becoming computerized. The online version of *Encyclopedia Britannica* is an excellent example of well-developed electronic reference tools that surpass the print version upon which they are based. The Library of Congress's American Memory project is an excellent source for historical maps, images, and primary documents. The best reference resources will continue to be developed in electronic formats; therefore, reference sections will not require the same amount of shelving in the future. Nearly all print periodical indexes, and many other reference indexes, have been replaced by electronic indexes. However, it is still quicker to look up the capital of Gambia in a print almanac than to log onto the Internet and do a search.

Fiction collections will likely grow. As literacy based instructional programs and integrated curriculum projects become more common, more teachers will be requiring students to read novels outside of the traditional language arts classes. Nonfiction collections will likely shrink as more information, particularly in the sciences, is gathered through the Internet and other online services.

Figure 3.3 Shelf Analysis

Type of Material	Present # of volumes	Present # of shelves	Present linear feet of shelving	Number of volumes to be shelved	Present anticipated growth/ reduction in collection	Volumes per linear foot	Number of linear feet/# of shelves needed
Reference Books							
Fiction Books							
Picture Books							
Easy Books							
000s							
100s							
200s							
300s							
400s							
500s							
600s							
700s							
800s							
900s							
Biographies/ Collective Bios							
Reserve Books							
Videos/DVDs							
TOTAL							

New Technologies

Do not think one can eliminate large parts of the collection. Although microforms and storage of back issues of periodicals have all but disappeared from most school media centers, it is difficult to curl up under a tree or in bed with a computer to surf the Web. Future formats to consider include electronic books and pod casting devices and the increased use of audio books and audio CD-ROM formats as well. Potential storage and check out of laptops, iPODs, PDAs, or other palm-sized computing devices may need storage space for loaners or spares if (or when?) the school moves towards a 1:1 computing ratio.

Aisle Width

When placing stacks, the width of aisles is an important consideration. Widths need to be great enough to accommodate wheelchairs (36 inches for a single wheelchair, 60 inches for two wheelchairs to pass according to ADA), but not take up more space than necessary. In some settings, where one may want to use the library media center for large group activities or have other reasons to need wide open spaces, ensure that the tables or other furniture can be slid between the stacks of shelving to create open areas. Moving tables between the stacks would require widths between the stacks of at least 44 inches if the school uses 42-inch square tables.

Visibility for Supervision

Another important issue regarding stack placement is visibility for supervision. It is important for the stacks to be placed in a manner that allows the library media center staff to see throughout the media center. In many cases, putting tall stacks along the perimeter walls, and using lower stacks in other areas of the library media center enhance both visibility and good space utilization. In cases where the collection size or available space does not allow for such stack placement, stacks can often be angled to allow good visibility from the circulation desk or another area where adult supervision is normally placed.

Display Shelving

In addition to the traditional spine-out shelving for print materials, it is wise to include some display shelving within the regular shelving areas. Display shelving can be used effectively where the fiction shelves meet the nonfiction shelves. Placing display shelving at the end of Dewey sections helps the students see the break and also provides a way to advertise materials. Display shelving can also be used within stacks close to the main entrance to market items as the students come in. Range end shelving is also becoming increasingly popular in all types of libraries. Such shelving allows for the easy display of materials on either shelving or hangers at the end of stacks.

For large collections, one may want to use such shelving to break up each range of Dewey numbers. However, do not include more display shelving than can be easily rotated by the library media staff so the displays do not get stale. If the students see the same displays in December that were present in September, they will quickly learn to ignore the displays. One might even want to try what some video stores are doing and display the favorite books of a given library media specialist, teacher, or administrator on a weekly or monthly basis. Some

display shelving can be purchased with built-in signage at the top or in the middle of the display. When developing displays, look to bookstores and video stores; both are focused on developing patron interest in their materials, as is a library media center.

Figure 3.4 Periodical Shelving

Closed Shelving

Traditionally, closed shelving included back issues of periodicals due to their fragile nature and the difficulties in replacing lost items. As full text databases replace the need for back issues of periodicals, other items have emerged to continue the need for closed storage. Closed stacks should include class sets of novels, videotapes, DVDs, CDs, PDAs, and laptops. If these materials are going to be requested regularly, make it a priority to place these stacks adjacent to the main service desk, unless staff at a separate service desk maintain the items in closed stacks. From a staffing perspective, maintaining two separate services areas is unwise unless the volume of traffic would require multiple staff members anyway.

When closed shelving will be placed directly behind the circulation desk, lift-up display shelving can be used to display current issues of popular periodicals and store back issues on the shelving below. Such shelving will give the circulation desk a cleaner looking backdrop than simple open shelving. Some shelving for audio-visual items

Figure 3.5 Extended Shelving

A Note on Compact Shelving:

Compact movable shelving has been used for storing textbooks and other closed stack materials in academic and special libraries for some time. More recently, it has started to be used by public and school libraries to address the issue of limited space. If the planning team determines that they would like to investigate high-density movable shelving, the first thing that must be done is that an engineer must determine if the building structure will be able to accommodate the additional structural load. In addition, the cost of such a shelving system may actually be more than simply adding additional floor space. Service and repair on the system will also be important, as the shelving will be expected to last from 15 to 20 years at a minimum. In elementary schools, such shelving would likely be too difficult for most students to use and could easily crush unknowing students when it moves.

can be built to allow the shelves to pull out like drawers. Drawers may allow for more shelves to be added to a single stand of shelving and can double the amount of storage available for DVDs and videos. Though not recommended for open shelving, if storage space is a severe problem, compact or high-density shelving (see box below) may be worth investigating for closed stack areas.

Student Seating

The time-honored rule about student seating used to be that the library media center be able to seat 10 percent of the student body. However, as the needs of students change, so has that rule. In many cases the number of library media specialists in the library media center determines the amount of available seating. As a general rule, have enough seating for one class for each library media specialist, plus one additional seating area. Using this guideline will provide for some drop-in traffic even if the library media specialist is working with a class. In cases where the library media center is fortunate enough to have more than a single, certified staff member, this rule will provide for each library media specialist to work with a class at the same time, plus still allowing for drop-in use.

In order to facilitate class use and drop-in use, it is important that each seating area be self-contained. Distinct class areas allow for both groups to use the center without interfering with one another. Figure 3.6 shows an elementary floor plan using shelving to assist in creating defined class areas. Figure 3.7 is a photo of the finished library media center.

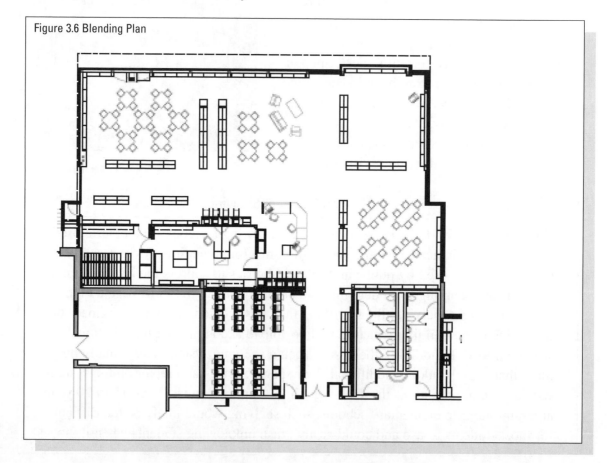

Figure 3.6 Blending Plan

Figure 3.7 Belinder Actual Photo

In planning areas for class use, always allow at least one more table than would be necessary for the largest classes regularly using the library media center. In most cases, if the largest classes contain 30 students, provide seating for 36. The extra capacity allows the classroom teachers to have a table that they can use to conference with students and organize materials while the other students conduct research or work with the library media specialist.

Seating at Tables

Seating is most often organized around tables. A common problem occurs in media centers when six or eight students congregate at a table designed for four. One of the best ways to reduce this problem is to use square tables instead of rectangular tables. Square tables can easily seat four students, but more students will have a difficult time working at one table. Rectangular tables can easily seat six students. Round tables are a third option, but they do not have the flexibility of being pushed together to make larger tables when necessary. For general seating, square tables are recommended. Some rectangular tables may be necessary if the students are often required to do large poster-sized projects and need the additional table space.

Table Shapes

In the library classroom or any area used primarily for direct instruction, narrow "testing" tables are a good fit. These narrow tables, meant for two people, are good for direct instruction. Students can be seated to all face in the same direction, and yet they can all have easy access to table space. In addition, this furniture arrangement can facilitate the development of a quiet study area when direct instruction is not taking place. Such an area is popular at the end of the grading period in most high school settings. The narrow testing tables can be moved together to form traditional rectangular tables.

Table Space

Planning space for traditional square table seating should be based upon 36 square feet per table. This is based on using 42-inch square tables with four chairs per table. This rule can be reduced for planning purposes to nine square feet per student needing seating. Seating 100 students would, therefore, require approximately 900 square feet of floor space. Using testing tables for seating will take up approximately the same space or possibly slightly more.

A Note on Tables:

When purchasing tables, address these basic issues. Tables constructed without stretchers between the legs will most likely survive longer, as the students will not use the support stretchers as foot rests. In modern construction methods, legs are also bolted to the tabletop itself, providing the same strength that glue and stretchers provided in the past. Generally, such tables are also easier to clean around because only the legs themselves will hinder the custodial staff. Square edges on tables facilitate sliding tables together to make larger surfaces. Beveled edges or bullnose edges are softer in case one bumps into the table, but leave a dip in the work surface when pushed together. For maximum flexibility, square edged tables are a better choice.

Another table topic is choosing laminate or solid wood tabletops. Generally, laminate tops are slightly more durable and easier to clean. It is also more difficult to carve into or mark up most laminates. Colored laminates allow a color scheme to be tied to tabletops, giving the library media center a more coordinated and colorful look.

Soft Seating

Comfortable leisure seating in library media centers is a nice addition for those students who want a spot to read a novel and a nightmare for the library media staffers who have to constantly remind students that they should not sit on the arms or have five students share the same chair. If the library has a need for soft seating, ensure that the seating is placed where it is easily monitored. In addition, choose furniture that cannot be easily moved by students. Heavy is a good thing when discussing soft seating. Heavy seating is not too difficult to achieve at the elementary or middle school, but those high school athletes will be able to move nearly anything. One should stick to chairs instead of loveseats and couches. Excluding couches and loveseats will help to eliminate the need to explain the "one per seat" rule to students who will argue that the couch can really seat many more than the media specialist thinks it can.

The Circulation or Service Desk

When the team has determined how much space will be needed to hold the collection and seat the student patrons, they can look to creating the circulation desk. Traditionally, it is here that much of the library's business is transacted. Students and staff check out their books and return them here. Now that the teaching role of the librarian has become more important with the advent of electronic resources and flexible scheduling, the circulation desk is no longer necessarily the focal point of the library media center, but it is still extremely important. The service desk generally has up to three functions. In a small library it may be used for circulation, reference, and as the library media specialist's desk. In a larger media center, these functions may be separated into three or more areas. First, determine what functions will be handled at the service desk.

Below, in Figure 3.8, are some of the functions that might be handled at the service desk:

Figure 3.8 Service Desk Functions

Function	Equipment or space needed
Check-in/check out of materials	Circulation computer, electrical outlets, network access, bar wand, de/magnetizer, book drop, space for loading book trucks from the drop, locking drawer for fine money, ADA access
Directional questions/Information	Good sight lines of the rest of the media center, posted hours and rules, space for supply storage
Retrieval of materials from closed stacks	Proximity to closed stacks, space to maintain records, IDs, etc.
Reference desk	Ready reference shelving, reserve shelving, phone books, phone, computer access, electrical outlets, network access
Media specialist's desk	Computer access, file storage, electrical outlets, network access, phone, printer

Once the team has determined the basic functions to be handled at the service desk, the library media specialist must delineate each function, how much equipment or space will be required, and any additional resources necessary for those functions to be performed. If possible, measure all of the equipment to determine how much space each requires. When measuring computers, leave a couple of inches on each side for access, and in the rear for the attachment of cables.

One should then have a library furniture vendor or an interior designer come in and draft a service desk design. The most basic designs for circulation desks are a "U" or a half circle. Some small library media centers have been built with a circular desk in the middle of the media center. Remember, circular designs generally will have less available storage than a rectangular or square desk design. When the team has a design that it is happy with, mock up the new service desk (in the new space if possible). Tape the basic perimeter of the desk on the floor, and then use existing furniture or even stacks of books to provide the height of the various sections of the desk. Remember that the height of the desk will need to be lower in elementary settings than in secondary schools. Walk around and examine the desk from all angles and determine if it will meet the identified needs for functionality and design. For specific desk and work surface heights and ADA compliance see Figure 3.9.

If designing the service desk for reference work, ensure that both the patron and the media specialist can easily see the computer screen at the same time. Where possible, the patron seeking reference services should be able to sit down next to the media specialist. Such a side chair would also make the space welcoming for a teacher who wants to sit down and speak to the media specialist; informal conversations produce some of the best collaborative lesson plans.

Figure 3.9 Work Surface Heights

Type of Work Surface	Height
Desk or sitting work surface (secondary student or adult)	29"
Desk or sitting work surface (middle school student)	27" to 29"
Desk or sitting work surface (elementary student)	25"
Keyboard tray (adult)	24"
Standing work surface (secondary student or adult)	34" to 37"
Standing work surface (elementary student)	30"
Desk or work surface (wheelchair compliant)	27"

Design the circulation or service desk to be not only functional but also welcoming. In most cases, the circulation desk will be the first thing that someone sees upon entering the library media center. If the library media specialist or an aide will be doing a good deal of work at the desk, provide raised sides or shelves to obscure the desktop itself. The desktop itself should be smooth and without raised joints, so that materials can be slid easily across the length of the desk. Ensure that the desk design or signs clearly point to where a student goes for assistance or to check out an item.

In large libraries, a second smaller desk for the support staff, or students who work at the desk, may be placed inside the main circulation desk. These desks should provide adequate space to process incoming periodicals, workspace for student workers, and adequate file and supply storage areas to supplement the main circulation desk.

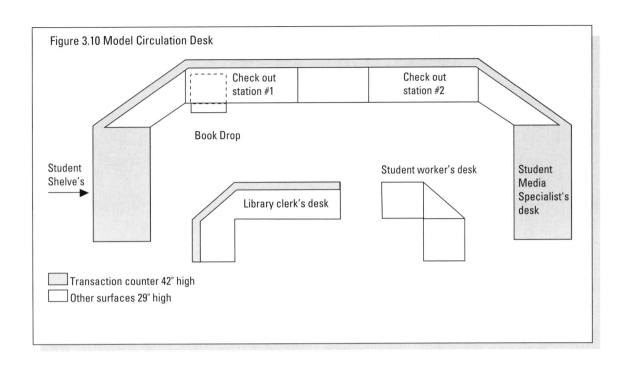

Figure 3.10 Model Circulation Desk

Check out station #1

Check out station #2

Book Drop

Student Shelve's

Library clerk's desk

Student worker's desk

Student Media Specialist's desk

Transaction counter 42" high

Other surfaces 29" high

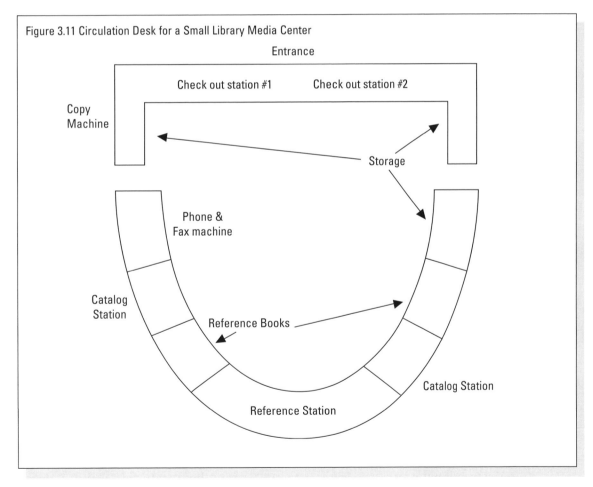

Figure 3.11 Circulation Desk for a Small Library Media Center

Entrance

Check out station #1

Check out station #2

Copy Machine

Storage

Phone & Fax machine

Catalog Station

Reference Books

Catalog Station

Reference Station

Figure 3.12 shows a blueprint for a circulation desk including the location for drawers, wiring grommets and leg spaces.

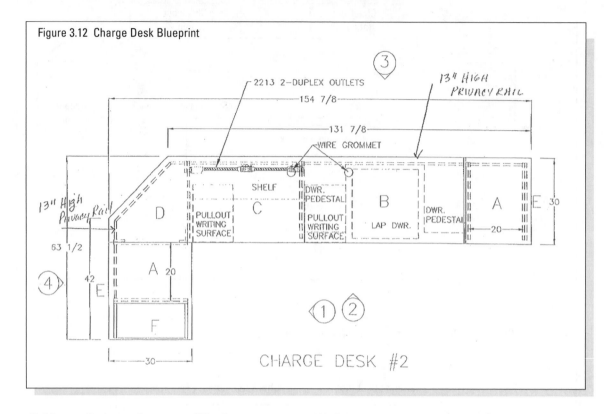

Figure 3.12 Charge Desk Blueprint

Microform Areas (if they are still in the collection)

Some secondary library media centers still have microform collections. If such equipment is in the media center collection, one must plan for how the materials will be accessed. In most cases, microfilm is the least susceptible to theft. Therefore, microform materials can be shelved in the open near the reader/printers for ease of access. The microform equipment can be placed out of high traffic areas unless it is a high use segment of the collection. Where possible, keep reader/printers and other equipment away from the entrance or any other place where there is security equipment. The electrical output of the systems can interfere with the effectiveness of the security system. In general, due to the rapid digitization of human knowledge, microform areas are not likely to need additional space in the future. Microform reader/printers can also be loud, so putting them near copy machines can limit noisy operations to one area. Such placement will keep both systems from interfering with security systems.

Conference Rooms

As instructional programs continue to evolve into the twenty-first century, the need for large and small group workspaces will continue to grow. The library media center has always been a place for students to research and work, and it will continue to be so. This need will require that the library media center be designed to include a number of small meeting rooms where groups can work without disturbing other patrons. In a small elementary school, only one such conference room is necessary, or an alcove could be designated for group meetings. In a large high school or middle school, two or three such conference rooms would help to support the instructional program. Place them in an easily supervised location and provide a telephone as well as access to the building network. In some cases, using glass walls or large windows into the conference areas can facilitate supervision.

Story Areas

The story area is one of the most important areas in an elementary media center. Where possible, a tiered story area is a wonderful addition to an elementary or middle school media center. It becomes a good place for a library media specialist to conduct "story time" with younger students. Such a tiered area can also be used for booktalks, large group, and whole class instruction. If light can be controlled, it can also be used for computer presentations and videos. With proper window treatments and lighting, this is an extremely effective section of a media center. Tiered areas should always go up and never be sunken. Sunken story areas are terrible hazards unless walled. Tiered story areas are ADA complaint as long as a wheel chair can be on the same level as some of the other students (e.g. the main floor level). There is no need to make each tier wheel chair accessible.

Audio Visual Production Area

Traditional Graphics

Library media centers will be providing traditional AV production services for the foreseeable future. Teachers and students still have to laminate, create transparencies, and erase old videotapes in a new facility. Elementary teachers will still need to use die cutting machines and bind student booklets as well. This area requires access to electrical outlets along a standing-height counter where teachers and students can work. Storage of the raw production materials, including colored paper, tapes, dies, and laminate should be on either open shelving or in locked cabinets, depending upon how the local school monitors supply usage. Because students are commonly asked to produce multimedia presentations and similar projects, have the team plan for the necessary additional storage space that will be required as such assignments continue to grow. The counter space should be able to easily hold a laminator, a paper cutter, and any additional equipment teachers are used to having access to. These types of AV equipment will need at least 24 inches of counter space each. Provide additional space for paper storage or any other supplies the media center will commonly stock.

AV Production Area for Traditional Graphics
AV equipment will need at least 24 inches of counter space. If possible, space for a photocopier for staff use should be included in or adjacent to the AV production area.

Electronic Graphics

The need for large dedicated production spaces for analog audio or video editing equipment depends entirely upon the library media program. Generally, if the team is building a new school, this space can be replaced with some reserved space in a computer lab. Here, digital technologies can be used to edit and incorporate audio and video into nearly any format, including back out to tape. In schools where a remodeling project incorporates a traditional audio/video production area, the team should already have a good idea of how much space such equipment requires. In addition, plan for enough additional space to incorporate computer-driven systems that may be added in the future. In a school with a broadcast quality radio or television program, look to the leadership in those areas to assist in determining their facilities needs.

Audio Visual or Other Equipment Storage

One of the most important areas in a library media center is where equipment is stored and repaired. When considering the fragile nature of most AV equipment and the increasing importance of its use in the classroom, storing this equipment in a hallway or other unsecured space is not wise. The amount of space necessary for this function depends on several factors including the amount of equipment permanently placed in classrooms, the amount of equipment available or planned for within the school, and the level of repair conducted in the building. If there will be a centralized media distribution system in the school, one will need less space than if the classrooms all must rely on mobile equipment. The equipment storage area should have a direct entrance from the hallway, and, if possible, be near an elevator in multistory buildings. This direct entrance should also be near the school's loading dock to facilitate equipment moving in or out of the building. Proximity to the library media staff is also important for security and checkout.

The storage area should have excellent lighting and good electrical and data wiring. It should have access to cable or a satellite hook up. In some cases, pre-programmed televisions and VCRs must be plugged in even when not in use or they forget their programming. This requires electrical outlets being placed along the entire perimeter of the room. It is also important to have adequate electrical outlets so equipment can be plugged in when personnel are troubleshooting or repairing equipment. Data network access will be similarly important if computer equipment is stored in this area. If all of the AV equipment in the school is on carts, shelf space will not be as important as floor space.

Place locked cabinetry liberally in this area. Some of the cabinetry should be designed with bins or small drawers for extra bulbs, small replacement parts, and the ever-present extra cables. Provide similar cabinetry for storing small pieces of equipment such as video cameras, digital cameras, and wireless microphones. For larger pieces of equipment, blank discs, and other less valuable supplies, open shelving can be used. If repair is to be done is this area, ample workbench space is crucial. In addition, provide secure storage for tools and adequate lighting. A phone ensures that a repairperson can talk to a technical support line and have the access to his tools and workspace. If possible, use speakerphones so the repairperson can still work while on-hold for technical support. Speakerphones are an easy way of improving the efficiency of repair staffs.

Computer Repair Spaces

As computers and related technology equipment become even more important in the educational process, on-site repair space is critical. Computer repair space should also contain multiple types of locking storage. Cabinets are necessary for the storage of network cards, extra memory, other spare parts, and tools required to repair computer equipment. Original copies of all software, spare equipment, and manuals must be stored securely. Repair bench space needs to be well lighted, have good electrical and data outlet access, have a speakerphone, and contain storage spaces appropriate for small items.

Open Storage Space

Open storage space for spare printers and computers is also important. Secure large equipment with some type of security cable system unless the room itself has a security system beyond a simple lock. If possible, this room should be near the AV storage and repair space, with access to an elevator and the loading dock. If located near computer labs or other technology spaces, the repair person can help to provide additional supervision in those areas from time to time. Design this space to handle the storage of new equipment when it first arrives until it can be set up in its permanent locations. However, because new equipment is not constantly arriving in most schools, space for new equipment should only be set aside in the largest schools. Old equipment that has yet to be disposed of or is being used as backup requires a secure place to be stored.

Network and Server Spaces

In addition to repair space for AV and computer equipment, network electronics and servers need high security spaces of their own. These spaces must be well secured and centered within the building, especially in small buildings to help control wiring costs and limit the need for intermediate wiring closets. Be sure to include adequate lighting, ventilation, and temperature control. The need to properly heat and cool these spaces is often overlooked because only equipment and not humans will be in the spaces. However, network electronics and servers like to be kept at a constant and reasonable temperature. At extremes, they tend to malfunction. Heating, ventilation, and air conditioning (HVAC) systems must account for the fact that network equipment needs consistent comfortable temperatures, and that much of the equipment also gives off heat.

Spaces for the main distribution frame (MDF) of the network need not be roomy, but they must allow for staff to easily reach all of the components to complete repairs, upgrades, and additional connections. Situate server spaces similarly so network administrators can easily get to equipment. In small schools,

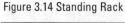

Figure 3.13 Wall Mounted Rack   Figure 3.14 Standing Rack

it would make sense to place any network devices within close proximity if the library media specialist will be responsible for network administration.

For some time, there was a move to provide Halon fire suppression systems in computer areas. However, Halon is no longer used in most cases, as it is a carcinogen, and water is now the suppression agent of choice in most systems.

Figure 3.15 Open Wiring Rack

Figure 3.16 Open Wiring Rack

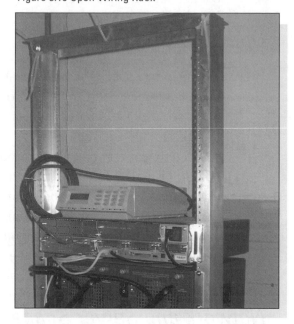

Within the wiring closets, there will need to be a variety of racks to mount network, telephone, and possibly video distribution equipment. Different types of wiring racks are used depending upon access non-network staff will have to the wiring closet. Open racks are the least expensive and provide the most access for technology staff. However, in spaces where students or other adults will have access, open racks are not advisable. One may mount closed racks on the wall or they can stand freely. Closed racks are a better option for spaces where non-network staff may be sharing the space. See Figures 3.13, 3.14, 3.15, and 3.16 for examples of electronics equipment racks in school settings.

Computer Spaces

Computers are essential tools for the modern library media center. Computers perform four functions within the library media center: catalog access, reference, student and staff productivity and multimedia production, and administration of the media center program.

Computers for OPAC (online public access catalog) access can be easily placed throughout the media center with several near the student entrance to the media center. These should be at standing height, with exception of those necessary for ADA requirements, so that students are encouraged to get their information and move on. Even if these stations can access other resources, standing height will provide greater access by having users spend less time at the stations. As a minimum, try to place one OPAC terminal for every 100 students in the school, plus one as a base. This number will work well in smaller schools (less than 500 students), but larger schools (over 1,000 students) may not need quite as many terminals, depending upon how students use their facilities at one time.

Access to electronic reference materials is a must within the school library media center. Locate several computers near the print reference collection that are primarily focused on providing access to reference resources. CD-ROMs, electronic versions of encyclopedias, atlases, and almanacs are all common examples of this type of resource. These machines must be tied into a building LAN, if one exists, and should have the highest level of Internet access available. Internet resources should be one type of resource provided, but access to only Internet resources would be limiting. The library media staff may also want to eliminate productivity software (word processing, spreadsheet, and presentation or database software) from these machines so they can be used exclusively for reference work. Eliminating such software may aid in preventing student plagiarism.

Productivity Software Access

One question is whether or not to provide access to productivity and multimedia production software on computers within the library media center. In small schools without other computer areas, it is essential that the library computers provide such access. In many cases, the library media center serves as a computer lab in addition to its information access role. In these cases, the access to multimedia development software, scanners, and the like is a primary part of the library media center. In larger schools where separate areas can be developed for multimedia and graphics production, duplication of such equipment in the library media center may be unnecessary. Similarly, in schools that have made a large investment in classroom technology and each classroom is already well equipped, the library media center space may be better used for other activities. If one is going to include productivity and multimedia production software within the milieu of the library media center, ensure that the facilities are near to any traditional production area. These areas need to have good access to adult supervision and assistance, and need to be structured so users can have a good deal of tabletop work area in addition to the computer resources.

In addition to the computers necessary for the users, the library media staff will have an ever-increasing need for good quality computer equipment. Where possible, let each member of the library staff have access to his own computer. These computers should all be on the building LAN and have Internet access. If this is not possible, provide the library staff with access to several workstations out of the way of patrons, either in the library office or in a workroom where they can work uninterrupted. Areas to work uninterrupted are especially necessary for the staff members working on adding new materials or cataloging. These tasks require a level of concentration not possible when surrounded by students or teachers in need of assistance.

The circulation desk also requires one or more computers for checking materials in and out, and a printer to easily print lists of charged materials or receipts. A fax and phone should also be available at the circulation desk. The only exception is if the fax machine is the only fax in the building. If so, the fax machine needs to be placed where students cannot read the incoming faxes.

Library Media Workroom

The library media center staff members need space to unpack new materials, hold books being mended, and keep supplies and book carts. This space can be behind the circulation desk, if enough space is available, or it can be a room near the circulation desk. The size of this room will vary depending upon the size of the library media staff. In a small school with only one staff member, such space may be unnecessary because when the staff member needs to work without interruption, the media center would have to be closed. In larger high schools, where the staff may approach the double digits, such space is essential. The technical processing of materials, if done locally, will in itself require a workroom. Sometimes one can locate a sink near the closed stack materials. This allows for the closed stacks to be run along the walls, and table or counter space can be left in the middle of the room for staff workspace. A sink is desirable in the workroom and allows for materials to be cleaned up without leaving the library media center. A sink is also helpful when the library media center is used for receptions or meetings that require coffee or food. Also include a lockable closet for coats and valuables in the workroom or office.

Library Media Specialist Offices

In some schools, the library media specialists want to have their own office space off of the main floor. Generally, this is a duplication of workroom space unless the school has a large staff. In most cases, if library media specialists are given their own space on the library floor, they will then be more accessible to students. If they conduct a meeting that requires them to be off the floor, they can use the workroom or one of the small group meeting rooms. In larger programs where there is a designated department head or director who supervises the rest of the staff, an office is necessary for the department head. In any case, provide all offices with good visibility and access to the main floor of the library media center. They should have adequate storage and shelving, and each office should be equipped with at least one phone and two network drops.

Library Media Staff Break Area

In many larger library media centers, a break area that doubles as a meeting area is useful. A refrigerator, a sink, and a microwave can be very valuable to any library media center from time to time. The sink mentioned above for the workroom need not be duplicated if the library media center includes a break area. Two small square tables could easily allow staff to take breaks in a comfortable area. In the same vein, the two tables could be pushed together for meetings with the staff or with other groups. Most library media specialists would also argue that it would be nice to include a washroom as well. A public washroom is especially important if the library media center will be open for extended hours when the rest of the school is closed off.

Archives

In some schools, the library media program is also required to serve as the school's archives. An archive is inherently different from traditional library spaces in that the materials stored are not necessarily intended for library use, and therefore require special handling and storage. Archival storage usually uses boxes and folders instead of traditional shelving patterns. If the library collects archival materials, ensure that proper storage and supervision can be included within the library media center. As archival areas tend to be open only for limited periods under direct supervision, the location of the archives in relationship to other areas of the media center is fairly unimportant. In some schools, the archives have even been put in a remote location to provide additional space for other functions within the media center. Whatever space is selected, it must be temperature and humidity controlled to protect the archival materials.

Putting the Pieces Together

Now that the team has determined areas and functions within the new library media center, the team must determine how the facility will be laid out. The layout can be done in a number of ways. In some cases, one may simply want to provide the architect the space and proximity requirements as set forth by the team in a manner similar to the table at the beginning of this section. After the architect has developed a basic layout, the team should review it and suggest modifications. In cases where the overall floor plan is predetermined by existing conditions or when the design timeframe is short, this method may be appropriate. This is often done with a bubble diagram that shows how spaces interact with each other. See Figures 3.17 and 3.18. Figure 3.17 is a bubble diagram from which Figure 3.18, an architectural drawing, was completed. Figure 3.19 is a photo of the computer reference area of the finished library.

Figure 3.17 Bubble Diagram

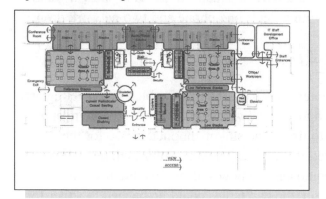

Figure 3.19 Computer Reference Area

Figure 3.18 Architectural Drawing

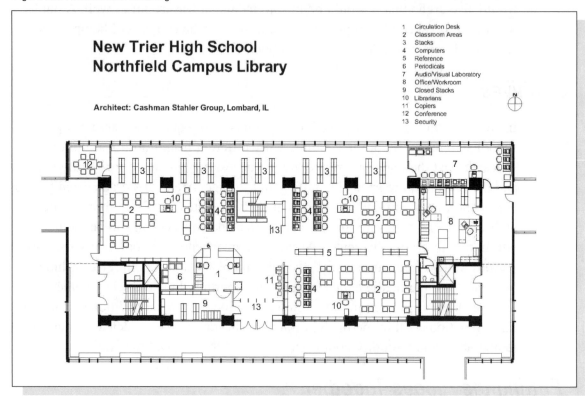

When working on renovation plans or simply replacing furniture in the library media center, drawings may come from a furniture supplier directly. These drawings often show a traditional floorplan view as shown in Figure 3.20. Many furniture or equipment vendors are also able to show a more 3-D perspective as shown in Figure 3.21. These isometric drawings show the top, front, and right sides of the layout. For many, this type of drawing makes visualizing the final library media center layout much easier. Figure 3.22 shows the story area of the library media center represented in Figures 3.20 and 3.21.

In other cases, the team may want to have two or three of the team members work directly with the architect to develop several possible floor plans that could then be presented to the entire planning team. This method will take longer but should provide a better end product if time and budget allow for the

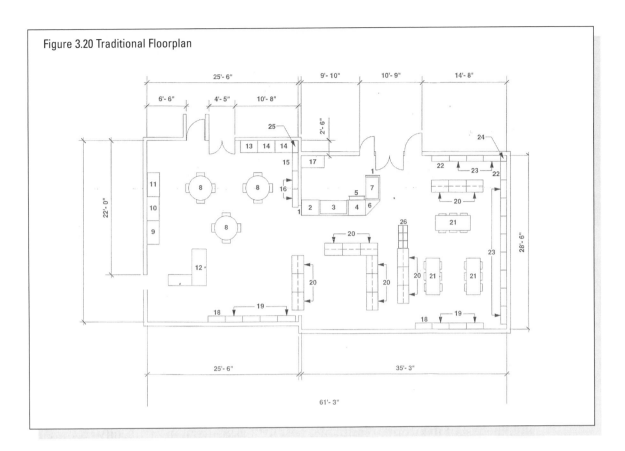

Figure 3.20 Traditional Floorplan

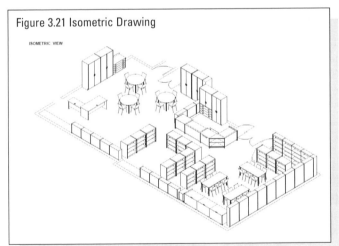

Figure 3.21 Isometric Drawing

Figure 3.22 Story Area of the Library Media Center

extra design time. Where possible, the planning team should do this design work within a library setting so the architect can easily see examples of the equipment or furniture being placed throughout the design. In this scenario, participants should include more than a single design so that the whole team can use the different layouts to compare and contrast features that they find effective or ineffective.

In some cases, one may have to eliminate or scale back the requirements of some spaces in order to fit more important areas into the design footprint. The team as a whole should discuss such plans. During the second phase, the whole team should determine what the library media center's needs are. In this phase, the team may prioritize, scale back, or eliminate some areas from the design in order to give more important areas the space necessary to function. It has been said that money is the final design criteria for architects. Most buildings would be different if the funds to build them had been unlimited. It is important for the design team to realize that space and funding will possibly require some compromise and scaling back from their original design criteria. However, the team should be careful not to compromise the functionality of one or more spaces just to allow another space to be added into the design. It is important for each area included within the final design to be functional in all ways. That does not mean that it needs to be perfect, but do not bother to include areas that are so limited in space or true functionality that they will never be useful.

For instance, if the team determines that two conference spaces are necessary in the second phase of the design process, do not demand two spaces if those spaces would end up the size of small closets. It would be better to have one truly functional conference room than two that would not provide functionality. In the same way, think about what areas can possibly be combined or overlaid upon other areas. Can the traditional AV production area be combined with the computer production area? Though there are no right answers for these questions, thinking through the possible combinations should allow the design team to come up with the best use of space.

Now that a basic design has emerged that the team is happy with, share it with the rest of the world. If possible, post the basic layout in the faculty workroom or dining room and invite people to make comments or suggest changes. Send the draft out to a number of other local library colleagues and ask for their input. Try to find some library media specialists who have recently done some renovation or building themselves; they will have thought through similar issues.

Fine-Tuning the Design

Once the team has determined the basic design, the details should assume center stage. One must work with the architect and the necessary specialists to determine the specifics for each area. If the design team did their job well in phase two, this process should not be too difficult. In each area, the team will choose the specifications for furniture and equipment specific to that area, the necessary electrical and networking outlets, lighting, and acoustics. In addition, the architect will determine the HVAC (heating, ventilation, air conditioning) and structural needs for each area of the media center.

LAMA (Library Administration and Management Association, an ALA division) suggests that the HVAC system be developed to provide no more than a 12 degree temperature variation throughout the year, using a base of 65 degrees. Such a temperature should allow the facility to maintain comfort for the patrons and staff as well as provide a safe environment for the collection.

Relative humidity should be maintained at approximately 40 percent for computers. When the relative humidity ranges above 60 percent, books and other print materials can be damaged by organisms that prefer a humid environment. In addition, high relative humidity can damage some types of computer-related equipment. High humidity will also cause paper supplies to jam copy machines and printers. Low humidity can cause a build-up of static electricity that can cause patrons to be shocked when using computers or other equipment.

Structural load is another important aspect of library media center facility planning. In areas of the media center, the floor is expected to hold a tremendous amount of weight. Load capacity is especially important in the stacks where weights of 150 pounds per square foot or more can be expected. In cases where the library media center has a second floor area used for shelving, ensuring that the structure can handle the weight of the stacks is critical. This can be especially true in remodeling projects, where the stacks are going to be significantly shifted. Before the team moves stacks, consult the architect or a structural engineer to help determine whether such a move is safe.

Furniture

Choosing the specific furniture the team desires for each area of the library media center is an important issue. In fact, library media center furniture can easily be required to have a natural life of more than 20, sometimes nearly 30 years of student use. Give proper time and importance to the development of bid specifications or selection of the furniture that the school will use in the library for the following decades. Two of the most important considerations for furniture must be *durability* and *warranty*. Find furniture that is easy to clean and maintain. Where possible, avoid textured surfaces or fabrics, which are difficult to maintain over time.

Chairs

A number of furniture vendors can provide well-made, plain wooden chairs in either four-legged traditional or sled-base designs. These chairs will serve particularly well over time in a high school environment, as basic wooden chairs are a nearly ageless style. If the team chooses a more contemporary or stylized chair, it might not look as good in 10 years as it does today.

Also try to avoid both tables and chairs with stretchers between the legs. These horizontal bars tend to make it difficult to clean under and around furniture, and provide an easy place for students to put their feet up. Older students can also break them off easily. Along the same lines, students rarely use the book tray under a chair, so do not order them; they simply become footrests. Also determine if the chairs need to be stackable if the library media center space is used for other functions, which will require additional floor space. If the team decides the library media center needs stackable chairs, look to models with lightweight plastic seats and backs, and tubular steel construction. In this case, ensure that the seats are firmly attached to the frame. In some chairs of this type, the seat can detach from the frame with enough pressure. This pressure can be as simple as leaning sideways or back on two legs if the user is heavy. Unfortunately, this tends to happen when an adult is using the chair, and the next thing one sees is a colleague on the floor looking up at them. Ensure that the chairs are sturdy enough for all users. Another issue is to try to avoid all sharp

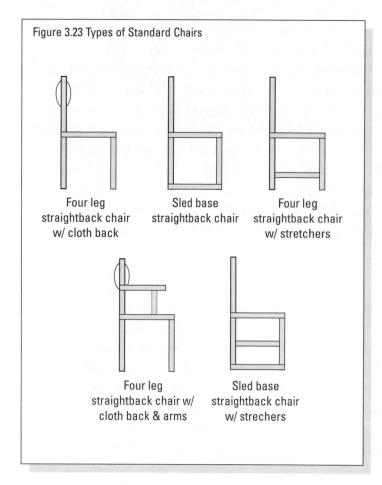

Figure 3.23 Types of Standard Chairs

Four leg straightback chair w/ cloth back

Sled base straightback chair

Four leg straightback chair w/ stretchers

Four leg straightback chair w/ cloth back & arms

Sled base straightback chair w/ strechers

Figure 3.24 Task Chair

Figure 3.25 Side Chair

metal edges and corners on chairs and shelving for obvious safety reasons. Sled chairs also work well for side chairs in offices because they easily can be slid around on tile or carpet. Most furniture companies have lines of chairs that have matching side chairs for task and management chairs.

Colors

Remember the avocado green refrigerators and harvest gold cabinets of the Brady Bunch era? For this reason, avoid using popular colors and look at tables with a laminate top that could tie into either wall or shelving colors. These tops tend to be more durable than plain wooden tops and are easier to clean.

Computer Furniture

When dealing specifically with equipment-related furniture, consider both power and wire management in choosing the appropriate furniture. In some cases, computer furniture is nothing but traditional furniture with grommets for wires and plugs drilled through the work surfaces. Remember to also plan for computers that may not be the exact size and shape of the computers that are used today. Though the Apple Macintosh series of computers have changed shape the most dramatically, personal computers have also changed shape from time to time. Choose computer furniture that allows multiple students to work together at a single computer station where possible. Today, many suppliers provide furniture with curved lines that can facilitate small group use of equipment. Computer furniture selection should be significantly influenced by its flexibility. In some cases, it might be simpler and more cost effective to design specific furniture and have a local cabinetmaker or millwork house build to the design. Such custom furniture can be designed as traditional furniture or as built-ins designed into the walls or other architectural features within the center.

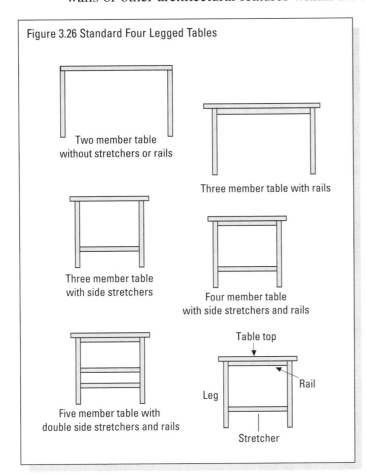

Figure 3.26 Standard Four Legged Tables

Two member table without stretchers or rails

Three member table with rails

Three member table with side stretchers

Four member table with side stretchers and rails

Five member table with double side stretchers and rails

Table top

Rail

Leg

Stretcher

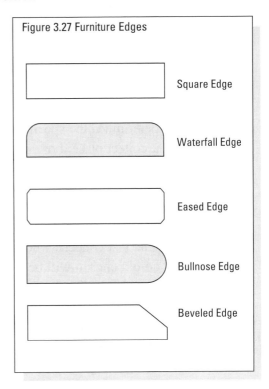

Figure 3.27 Furniture Edges

Square Edge

Waterfall Edge

Eased Edge

Bullnose Edge

Beveled Edge

In selecting furniture, never look to only one vendor. In most cases, vendors will be glad to bring in samples of different types of chairs, so try them out. With task chairs, find out if the same model can be ordered with and without armrests. Using two versions of one chair as opposed to two different models could help develop a single large order instead of two smaller orders. Ordering in quantity will generally help keep down the price and make installation easier because one will have fewer vendors to deal with. It can be very difficult to develop furniture specifications without assistance, so the team may want to choose specific brands and models. Be sure that the team reviews applicable board policies regarding developing specifications and bid practices. In most cases, multiple vendors will carry a line of furniture in the area so this should not affect the bid process. In addition, if one is comfortable with the concept, one may specify a model and allow an "equivalent" model to be bid. This allows for a greater range of bidders, but may not get the team the furniture desired. Some states require the "or equivalent route" to provide for more open ended bidding. Some districts do not allow for any specific item or brand to be specified. The method the team uses in bidding equipment should be reviewed with the business manager who will be able to provide guidance.

Furniture Arrangement

When trying to determine what will or will not fit into a specific area, develop a grid system to try out various furniture arrangements. By using a scaled grid on either paper or a magnetic sheet, one can easily manipulate potential furniture arrangements. Using a scale version of the center will allow furniture to be arranged and then checked to ensure that aisle width and ADA access needs have been met. At least one manufacturer of library and computer furniture provides a magnetic board and scale versions of their furniture when working with customers. This process allows one to really look in depth into each area of the media center. It ensures that furniture and equipment will fit into the area while still leaving the necessary room for patrons to use the spaces effectively. When the team has determined the specific furniture and equipment layouts for each area, have the architect place those into a set of drawings. From this set of drawings, one can now look to the specific electrical and data networking needs of each area.

Enduring Styles

One last concern when deciding on furniture is whether or not the styles or colors chosen will be available next year or in 10 years. Some manufacturers will be able to tell one if a style is being phased out or if the style is a core product that the company plans to continue for many years. Due to the nature of some government contracts, the company may even be required to maintain replacement parts for a certain furniture line for a number of years. If the LMC being designed may be expanded in the future, the ability to add matching furniture may be a desirable option.

Steps in Creating Bid Documents

1. Determine general needs in each area.
2. Determine specific equipment and furniture required.
3. Specify functions of furniture and equipment for bidding.
4. Determine electrical and data and other infrastructure needs.
5. Draft architectural plans.
6. Approve architectural plans.
7. Draft bid documents and determine alternatives.
8. Approve final bid documents.
9. Release bids.

Figure 3.28 is a sample furniture bid including both library and computer workstation furniture products.

Figure 3.28 Furniture Bid Specs

| | | Names and phone numbers of department administers will be distributed at the mandatory pre-bid meeting scheduled for 2:00pm, Wednesday, September 20, 2010, Room 104 (Board Room) at East Campus, 100 W. Brainard Ave., Balltown. | | | |

Depart ment	Quanity	Description	Manufacturer	Model #	Total Bid Price
CAREER CENTER					
		Sample: Invincible Office Furniture			
	1	Workstation - including:			$
		AMCD22 - Center Drawer 24"w x 22 3/8" x 2"h			
		TL48UM - Task Light 44"w - 30 watts			
		TL60UM - Task Light 56"w - 32 watts			
		V2820BL - Freestanding Ped Box/Box/File w/lock 15"w x 28"d			
		VCM19 - Task Light Cord Manager (2)			
		VCT4830KB - Corner Section 48"w x 30"d x 29"h w/AKB, Clear L&R, T-edge			
		VT5430LER - 54"w x 30"d x 29"h Clear Left/Full Right, T-edge			
		VT6630LER - 66"w x 30"d x 29"h Full Left/Clear Right, T-edge			
		RDBR54L - RDU/Riser Overhead cabinet w/lck 54" x 15" x 35 1/2"h			
		RDBR66L - RDU/Riser Overhead cabinet w/lck 66" x 15" x 35 1/2"h			
	1	V542L - Vista 5 drawer lateral file w/lock 68"h x 42"w x 19 3/8"d			$
	2	V536L - Vista 5 drawer lateral file w/lock 68"h x 36"w x 19 3/8"d			$
	2	V442L - 4 drawer lateral file w/lock 55"h x 42"w x 19 3/8"d			$
	1	Workstation - including:			$
		TL48UM - Task Light 44"w - 30 watts			
		TL60UM - Task Light 56"w - 32 watts			
		V2820BL - Freestanding Ped Box/Box/File w/lock 15"w x 28"d (2)			
		V2820FL - Freestanding Ped File/File w/lock 15"w x 28"d			
		VCM 19 - Task Light Cord Manager (2)			
		VCT4830KB - Corner Section 48"w x 30"d x 29"h w/AKB, Clear L&R, T-edge			
		VT3630LER - 36"w x 30"d x 29"h Clear Left/Full Right, T-edge			
		VT3630LER - 72"w x 30"d x 29"h Full Left/Clear Right, T-edge			
		RDBR48L - Overhead cabinet w/lock 48" x 15" x 35 1/2"h			
		RDBR72L - Overhead cabinet w/lock 72" x 15" x 35 1/2"h			
		V236L - 2 drawer lateral file w/lock 27 1/4"h x 36"w x 19 3/8"d (3)			
	1	Workstation - including			$
		AMCD18 - Center Drawer 18"w x 22 3/8"d x 2"h			
		AKB Articulated Keyboard Tray 21 3/4" x 10 1/2", Nylon			
		BS48HS - Bookshelf, high sidd 16 1/2"h x 48"w x 15"d			
		HWT48 - Single Wall Track for RDU & bookshelf 16 1/2"h x 48"w			
		TS60 - Transaction Shelf 60"w x 15"d x 13"h, t-edge			
		V2220BL - Freestanding Ped Box/Box/File w/lock 15"w x 22"d			
		V2220FL - Freestanding Ped File/File w/lock 15"w x 22"d			
		VCT3624B - Corner Section 36"w x 24"d x 29"h, Clear L&R, T-edge			
		VT3024LER - 30"w x 24"d x 29"h Clear Left/Full Right, T-edge			
		VT6624ELR - 66"w x 24"d x 29"h Full Left/Full Right, T-edge			
LIBRARY					
		Sample: Beckley Cardy/School Specialties			
	1	AM2436NPP - Computer table with laminate top - 24" x 36"			$
	1	2403AB10N - Guest chair			$
	2	792L-P - 2 drawer lateral file w/lock - 42" wide			$
	1	519483 - 84" laminate top for lateral files			$
	1	38155 - 30" x 60" double pedestal desk			$
	1	P84962 - 30" x 60" double pedestal desk - w/locking drawers			$
	1	46C- Wood Bench - 48" x 18" to match wood & fabric of existing chairs			$

DISCOVERY CENTER					
		Sample: Spectrum Industries			
	2	38670 KP - Computer Desk 36"w x 30"d x 27"h			$
	1	38666 KP - Desk 30"W x 30"d x 27"h w/o slot			$
	24	38678 KP - Computer Desk			$
	4	38678 KP - Computer Desk 60"w x 30"d x 27"h			$
	1	38673 KPADJ - Computer Desk 44"w x 30"d x 27"h			$
TECHNOLOGY COR					
		Sample: Beckley Cardy			
	1	Workstation - including:			$
		VTC4230 - Corner desk unit 42" x 30" x 29"h			
		AKB - Keyboard tray w/mouse pad			
		AMCD-18 - Pencil Drawer 18"			
		VT4830 - Left Desk Return Unit 48" x 30"			
		V2220-BL - Freestanding Ped Box/Box/File w/lock 15"w x 22"d			
	2	V242-L - 2 drawer lateral file w/lock 42"			$
	1	7701-AB62 - Task chair - fabric w/arms			$
	1	LED-L423WT - Lamp w/22" reach			$

The team's furniture specifications are now complete. If possible, keep a binder of the specification sheets for each of the furniture items that is chosen, the color swatches or samples for each item, and the layouts that were completed for each area. In the front of the binder also include the total number of each item to be ordered and the suggested retail cost so that one can create and update an accurate furniture budget. This binder will aid greatly the business office in streamlining the development of the bid specifications for the furniture.

Electrical and Data Networking Needs

Data needs may be the single most difficult aspect to plan. The state of the art of networking is a fluid target. Planning for networking that will be sufficient in five years, not to mention that life expectancy of a school, is nearly a mind-boggling task. The last section reviewed the importance of choosing furniture that will last for 20 or more years. Trying to plan three to five years ahead in technology is difficult. Planning 20 years ahead for technology is like trying to put out a house fire with a squirt gun. Sure it can be done, but the success rate is not inspiring.

The easiest way to approach this task is to determine where every piece of equipment and computer will sit within the library media center. When this determination is made, one can easily provide enough electrical outlets for the opening of the media center. In addition, do the same with the data and voice drops. Every desktop computer and printer gets a data drop. A data drop is the outlet or jack that allows a connection between the computer and the network, much like one has a phone outlet at home to connect the phone. In the same manner, ensure each library staff workstation has at least two data drops per user, unless there is a large office space where one voice and one data drop for each user plus one extra of each will be sufficient. Also plan for two data drops for each photocopier or other device. The photocopiers are evolving into large network printers and fax machines; in fact, many already are capable of such multifaceted roles. Remember that when one is planning renovation or construction, the cost of installing an electrical and networking backbone is much less than if one has it done later, so wire for the future.

The one area that is difficult to predict is the wiring necessary for student seating areas. You can look at this in two ways. The first way is that as students start to bring their own laptop computers into the school, they will need to connect to the building network and access an electrical outlet while working in the library media center. This is a fairly safe assumption based upon today's laptop. However, the second philosophy towards student computers or PDAs is that those devices will have batteries necessary to power the device for the school day and that the devices will be able to connect to the school's network via well placed wireless access points. Emerging technologies appear to be close to the $100 laptop for students. The second planning guide for providing for wireless access without cabling for student computers is the more reasonable path. Providing additional power outlets throughout the library media center is recommended.

In addition, effective wireless networks that will allow students to connect to the school network without having to plug into a network drop are ubiquitous today in hotels, airports, and coffee shops. Soon most schools will have them. If the design team wants to plan for the adoption of wireless networking within the library media center, but not an installation at the time of construction, one should provide some electrical and fiber drops within the ceiling so that the wireless hubs can be put easily in place in the future without having to provide additional wiring at that time. To be safe, plan for some electrical and data drops at a few of the student seating areas. Remember that large copy machines and presses often have more demanding power requirements than a standard electrical outlet can provide. One should check with the vendor regarding the specific power and data requirements of any large pieces of equipment.

Wiring Options

Copper Options

Unshielded twisted pair (UTP)
- Category 3 (voice quality only)
- Category 5 (least costly data option)
- Category 6 or 7 or Gigabit (possible long term data advantages over Cat 5)

Shielded twisted pair (STP)
- Generally used in older Token Ring networks; thicker than UTP; not generally used today.

Fiber

- Multi-mode fiber is generally used in data networks. It costs more than copper as does its support system. It can be used as a backbone between hubs of a copper network. Single mode fiber, traditionally used for video application, is beginning to be required for some gigaspeed networking backbones. It is wise to include both types of fiber if the budget can handle the cost.

Wireless vs. Wired Networks

Before the design team agrees to an entirely wireless solution, there should be a thorough review of the advantages and disadvantages of wired versus wireless networking. Making a wireless network secure is a much more difficult task than managing a wired network and consideration must be given to the methods and costs of such security. The design team will also need to work with the technology staff to ensure that the right protocol is chosen for the intended use of wireless within the school. The Institute of Electrical and Electronic Engineers (IEEE) has defined several wireless standards. The design team should ensure that the technology staff chooses the most appropriate type of wireless equipment. Security concerns may also direct a school or district to retain wire networks for phone services even if the phone system is a voice over IP system (VOIP).

For more information on wireless networking in schools refer to the following Web sites:

- A Guide to Wireless LANs in K-12 Schools <www.cosn.org>
- Aruba Networks <www.arubanetworks.com>
- 3 Com Networking <www.3com.com/solutions>
- Network Startup Resource Center (designed for the Third World, but very informative) <www.nsrc.org/wireless.html>
- Wikipedia Article on 802.11 <en.wikipedia.org>
- Wireless Design Online <www.wirelessdesignonline.com>

Figure 3.29 A Data Drop

Cabling

Deciding what type of cable to pull is another discussion that the design team and technical staff should have. Today there are three basic wiring options, category 5 copper (UTP), gigabit or level 7 copper (UTP), or fiber. UTP stands for unshielded twisted pair. This is opposed to STP, shielded twisted pair, which is often used in older Token Ring networks. The three options presented assume one has an Ethernet-based network. If the school or district is using Token Ring or another protocol, see the school's vendor about suggested wiring options. In all cases, a fiber backbone between wiring closets should be the standard. The advantages of category 5 or "cat 5" cable are the relatively low cost of both the wire and the computer's network or NIC cards. Copper wire is fairly standard throughout the country and can easily handle 100MB Ethernet networking.

Gigabit (level 7) copper is more expensive than cat 5, but it is designed to try to "future proof" the network without the cost of fiber installation. Though one should realize that no network installation can be future proofed, gigabit copper provides a potentially larger bandwidth without the cost of fiber. Gigabit networking protocols are already materializing, but the need for a gigabit data pipeline into the average elementary classroom has not yet materialized.

Fiber is the most costly option because both the fiber itself and the NIC cards necessary to connect computers to fiber tend to be more expensive than copper options. In some cases, schools have chosen to pull several fiber and several copper to each classroom. Generally speaking, these were cases of overkill. Remember that one can always plug a hub into the data jack and instantly add additional connections, though one may sacrifice some speed in doing so.

Another issue with data and electrical placement is the ability to group the drops by pairs or quads to lower the overall cost of faceplates for the jacks. If the data and electrical drops can always be put in pairs or quad groupings, the overall cost of the project can generally be lowered. In lab settings, one may be able to place data drops in groups of six. However, because power cables tend to be fairly standard in length, the electrical outlets should still be in fours. By the same token, the cost to install a single data or electrical outlet makes it wise to always install at least two jacks in a location. Do not plan for only one network drop for a projection device at the rear of the library classroom. The planning team should specify two drops. The cost will be fairly similar, and one will have an extra drop for an unforeseen future need.

As with furniture selection, the architect, electrical engineer, or network consultant should provide drawings showing the location of each electrical outlet and network drop. Include voice (phone) jacks within the network drop. In collaboration with the technology staff of the building or district, specify exactly what type of connectors, cable, and wire mold will be used throughout the library. If the media center is to be wired for the first time, ensure that the technology coordinator or network manager has developed a labeling scheme for the network's data and phone outlets that can be understood easily and included within the bid specifications for any cabling work. In addition, ensure that the labeling of all data and phone outlets is done by machine. Do not allow the installers to label the outlets by hand. In two years, it would be difficult to tell whether the installer had scribbled an "E," "F," or "G" on the faceplate. If the labels are printed on a computer, this problem will not occur.

Conditioned Power

Regarding power itself, most computer professionals will ask that new buildings include "conditioned power" for computers and other electrical devices. Such power is "cleaner" and less likely to cause hardware problems due to power variances. In many building projects, orange outlets signify such conditioned power. You should discuss the need for conditioned power with the technology staff and the project's electrical engineer.

Lighting

The design team must attend to lighting and visibility for the new center as well. All too often, a library media center has problem areas where it is either too bright or too dark during certain times of the day or in certain weather conditions. Lighting must be considered for each area of the library media center individually, as well as for the overall facility. Little has been done to determine the best methods of lighting educational settings. However, there is general agreement that the method of illumination can affect the educational environment. The amount of illumination is a primary issue, but several other issues are also important.

The ability to vary the amount of illumination within a given space is essential. This is especially true in areas where computer projected images are being used. Three basic types of illumination are used in schools: natural light, direct artificial light, and indirect artificial light. Direct artificial light is the most commonly used lighting source in schools, though many feel that this is the least desirable. A mixed lighting solution that relies on multiple forms of illumination is generally preferred.

Natural Lighting

Natural lighting should be included in the lighting scheme when possible. However, natural light is generally unreliable. The sun never seems to shine in the windows when one wants it to, and that same sun can bring with it a terrible glare through a western window in the late afternoon. Southern exposures tend to provide the brightest natural light sources during the middle of the day, while northern exposures tend to provide more consistent lighting throughout the day. In areas that get a good deal of sun, planners should consider windows on northern exposures that let less heat and light inside. Where windows are included on both the northern and southern exposures, provide fewer or smaller windows on the southern exposure to balance the overall amount of natural light allowed inside. If areas are going to be used for presentations with video projectors or LCD panels, one will need to install shades or blinds in order to darken the area enough for such presentations to be effective. Because of the possible interference of natural light with computer-generated presentations, skylights should be avoided in those areas. However, skylights might be appropriate in areas designated for leisure reading, where class presentations are unlikely.

Lighting Placement

When determining the placement of lighting in an area, try to ensure that each probable instructional area can be controlled separately. The best situation is to be able to control the lighting in a given area completely. There should be no light pollution from one area into any other in a "perfect" design. Light pollution is addressed in a number of ways. The first is to ensure that at least one of the light banks installed in each instructional area can be dimmed. Dimming allows for more variable lighting than if each bank of lights can only be turned on or off. A second method is to install the regular florescent lights and then add a second set of can lights that can be controlled with a dimmer. In areas that have been remodeled to be used primarily for computer presentations, adding indirect lighting in the form of floor lamps to an existing lighting scheme can provide more variability in lighting than would be available in a tradition classroom. Wall sconces provide indirect lighting and can also serve a decorative purpose.

Positioning the lighting is particularly important in several areas. In the open stack section of the library media center, lighting is extremely important if patrons are to be able to browse the stacks easily. Such lighting should run parallel with the shelves. If lights run perpendicular to the shelves, they tend to throw more shadows than if the lights are directly above the aisles. Presentation areas have specific lighting requirements. Lighting for display cases or wall art should also be considered. Halogen spotlights work well for illuminating wall art and other objects of interest within the library media center. Ensure that all exits are brightly lit for safety and security.

Glare is the amount of light that reflects into the eye. Indirect lighting generally produces less glare than direct lighting. Visual comfort is the ease of seeing, based on fixture design and placement. Visual comfort is also impacted by the amount of contrast and ceiling colors. Colors best suited to enhance visual comfort are ivory, white, light beige, and pale yellow.

Lighting and the Security System

Most artificial lighting can also create an electrical and magnetic field (EMF). While generally thought to be benign, EMF can affect some library security systems. Before deciding on a library security system, be sure that it will function within the EMF range created by the lighting, copy machines, and computers being used. It is not good planning to design a media center where the security system does not work when the lights are turned on.

Exit and Emergency Lighting

In addition to general lighting issues, ensure that the media center has the necessary exit lights and emergency lights in case of fire or other emergency. Check with the architect or the local fire marshal for specifics, but these types of lights are normally required at all exists, stairways, and restrooms. Night lights may also be necessary for the media center depending upon where it is located within the building, and the length of any interior corridors and stack areas. In every case, try to locate the switches for all of the lights in one central area, near the entrance most likely used by staff in the morning. The only lights that should not be included in this area are those that are likely to be turned on or off regularly to support presentation needs. Lights used for presentations must be controllable from the areas they illuminate.

Acoustics and Noise Reduction

Where possible, the team should isolate each area of the library media center from the noise of the other areas. One of the best noise reducers is carpet. If at all possible, carpet the media center. If there will be a direct outside entrance to the library media center, the team should provide a small tiled entry way for people to remove shoes or boots in bad weather, but carpet is the best first step towards an acceptable noise level in the media center.

In addition to the floor, many wall coverings, especially those that are fabric based, can absorb sounds and reduce noise levels. Fabric covered display boards and shelving end panels can also absorb sound. The shelving and the books themselves can help keep sound from traveling from one area of the library media center to another. In cases where the team cannot sacrifice lines of sight for noise reduction, consider glass walls or partitions.

When designing spaces, keep the high noise activities, like the computer production areas and the circulation desk, away from the areas that will be used for library media specialist presentations and other direct instruction, like the library classroom areas. Some copy machines and microform printers will also fall into the noisy equipment category. Do not allow equipment noise to detract from the overall atmosphere of the media center. When questioned as to why he did not use the library media center, a teacher responded that the computers and printers made too much noise and distracted his students from their reading. When that media center was redesigned, the computers were moved from the middle of the media center to one side. On the opposite side were the fiction stacks and a class seating area that the language arts teacher in question used almost weekly the following year. Try to obtain feedback from the end users constantly during the design process. Such feedback will result in a more effective library media program.

Color and Design

Though the design team is not expected to have the talents of an interior designer, it is important to try to make the new library media center look friendly and inviting. Color is amazingly important in setting the tone in a library media center. Elementary schools should choose bright crisp colors particularly pastels or the school's colors. Secondary schools should try to stick with the school's colors that will stand the test of time. Avoid red and bright yellows and oranges. These colors tend to excite people and colors with a more calming effect are often better in the school library media center.

In the same manner, lighter wood stains like natural oak or maple will tend to open up the library media center where darker wood stains, like cherry or mahogany, will make the library media center appear smaller and less inviting. Using standard light or medium oak stains will also allow the district to move furniture between schools as enrollment shifts student population without creating a patchwork look.

Choose one or two core colors, a wood stain, and possibly one or two accent colors to be used throughout the media center. It is a simple task to have the furniture and shelving vendors provide color choices and to have them match the colors of other vendors where necessary. Where possible, the colors should be basic and based upon the school colors or some other combination that will not become obsolete in a few years.

One library media center used a light blue base for the shelving with a dark blue accent stripe and a dark blue carpet. The task chairs were dark blue or wine along with the bulletin boards, signs, and the colors integrated into the service desk panels. The walls were an off-white and gray. Gray was also used for cabinetry, some shelving, and the laminate inset of the student tables. The tables themselves were a light oak as were the chairs and the end panels of the stacks.

Try to avoid large murals on walls where directional signs need to be placed. Busy murals tend to create activity and movement and do not provide a calming impact on students either. Patrons often overlook signs that are on the wall within or near a mural.

If the team is required to reuse existing furniture, contact a painter who can use electrostatic painting techniques to transform the old metal furniture so that it fits into the new color scheme. Electrostatic painting is a simple and inexpensive process for any metal furniture, desks, or file cabinets. Even old bookends can be repainted to look like new. If the design team feels that they have no flair for color, contact one of the furniture vendors who has an interior designer on staff or go down the hall and enlist the help of an art or family and consumer science teacher. Some architectural firms also provide interior design services.

Signage

The last important aspect of the library media center design is signage. If at all possible, leave the development of a signage pattern until the new furniture has been installed and the space has been used for at least a couple of months. Use temporary signs in the interim. Temporary signs will allow monitoring of how the space is actually used, how the traffic patterns form, and where and what directional questions are asked. A number of different types of signage are necessary in the new or renovated library media center.

Directional Signs

Directional signs tell the user where to go for a service or a resource. The entrance and exit signs are the basic directional signs. Some library media centers will also want to use signs to help manage traffic flow within the media center or to inform users about doors they should not use.

Room and office signs designate staff offices and will help inform patrons what goes on within a given space. In school library media centers, many of these signs will also state "Staff Only" or "Teachers Only." In cases where the name on the door may change before the sign will, most companies have a series of signs that include both permanent and temporary signs.

Location Identification

Location signs will point out the circulation desk, the reference area, the copy machines, the microform area, and the story area. These tend to be larger signs that can be easily read from both the entrance and the circulation desk. Many times signs can be mounted high on a wall or hung from the ceiling. Do not use too many direction signs; the media center staff can always direct a student to another area, by saying "just past the reference area sign are the story collections."

Collection Signage

Developing proper signage for the print collection is essential. The stack end signs should be of the nonpermanent type, so that as the collection size changes or interest in topics grows or wanes, the signs will not have to be replaced. The signs can be created so that the call number ranges can easily be changed without problem. Of course, the students will have difficulty with the stacks until the signs are placed, so prepare for a semester of yellow notes on the ends of the new stacks.

Place informational signs by the entrance to broadcast announcements, state hours, or illuminate rules. Informational signs near the copy machines, computer printers, and AV equipment may also be useful in the media center.

Signs, as other areas of the library media center, will need to meet ADA requirements. ADA requirements encompass height requirements for certain signs and Braille letters on the signs. In addition, look to use standard symbols and icons where possible. Use consistent language throughout all signage. Also use simple understandable terminology. Ensure that the colors of the signs compliment the overall color scheme of the media center, stand out, and are easy to read from a distance. Use both upper and lower case lettering in the signs. All upper case letters are more difficult to read than a mix of both. Use sans serif fonts; such fonts are easier to read at a distance. Use high contrast color schemes for the lettering and background of the signs.

Now that the design team has completed the planning stage of the facilities design process, the architect and business manager can develop construction documents and bid documents for the new or renovated library media center. Some districts will also want a lawyer to review the bid documents before they are released to perspective bidders. The design team should review the plans before the business office and architect let them out to bid. This review should ensure that everything has been properly translated from the plans to the bid documents. As changes occur, and they will, it will be important for the design team to keep in contact with the architect, and later the general contractor or construction manager, in order to assure that the project is going according to plan. Remember, throughout the building process be sure to "supervise, inspect, and revise."

Chapter 4

Computer Lab Spaces

In addition to the computers in library media centers, the planning team must develop plans for any computer lab spaces. Educators continue to fluctuate on whether computers should be placed within lab settings or distributed within classrooms. Both concepts have merit, and in a perfect setting the school would have both. Computers would be placed within each classroom, and the school would have at least one lab where an entire class could go for direct instruction. In larger schools with computer-based curricular offerings, a computer lab is essential. In other schools, the lab might be part of the library media center providing drop-in or before and after school access for students.

The first design decision in a computer lab is whether it will be used primarily for direct instruction or for individual or small group drop-in. If direct instruction is to be a major or even moderate part of the lab's use, design the lab to support direct instruction. It is extremely difficult to teach computer-based classes and keep students on task. Assist the teachers by providing them with a facility that can both support them and encourage student focus.

In computer labs where direct instruction will be a major focus of the facility, ease of access to each student station and good sight lines are key issues. In all labs, storage is also a significant issue. In addition to storing computer supplies, there is a need to store student backpacks, bags, and notebooks. Several basic layouts are available when working with computer lab spaces. When possible, spaces that are roughly square are preferred over spaces that are rectangular in shape. Long narrow spaces tend to spread student stations out, so that the rear of the lab is fairly well removed from both the teaching station and any projected images at the front of the room. In addition, these long narrow spaces tend to turn the instructor into a track star because the students with questions will invariably be in the last row of the computer lab.

For direct instruction computer labs, the traditional row design is an option. This layout has the computers placed in front facing rows with a center aisle. Wiring is easy because it can emanate from the walls and does not require boring through the floor or erecting power poles. When multiple aisles are added, wiring has to be modified to come up from the floor or down from the ceiling. There are advantages to such a layout.

1. Good lines of sight for students in lecture.
2. Students can view the board, projected images, the teacher, and their computers simultaneously.
3. The teacher easily can see all of the screens by walking to the rear of the room. With the addition of a remote mouse and a laser pointer, the teacher can watch the screens and teach at the same time.
4. Wiring is extremely simple with a single central aisle.
5. Furniture to support this layout is easy to obtain.

There are disadvantages to the traditional row layout as well.

1. Not designed for student collaboration or group work.
2. Teacher access to students sitting on the inside of rows is difficult.

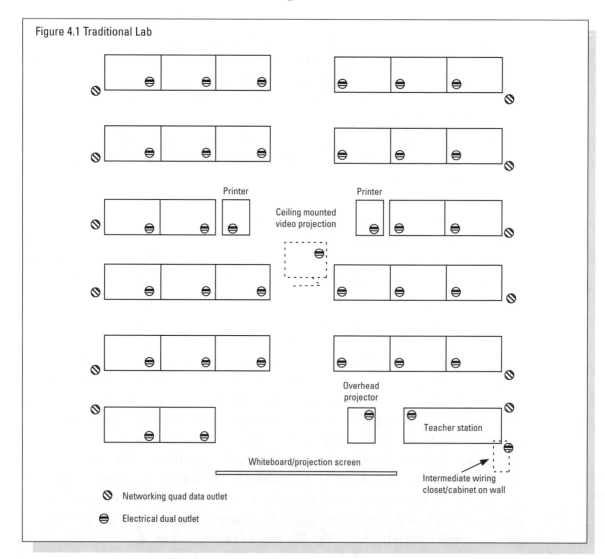

Figure 4.1 Traditional Lab

Printer

Printer

Ceiling mounted video projection

Overhead projector

Teacher station

Whiteboard/projection screen

Intermediate wiring closet/cabinet on wall

⊘ Networking quad data outlet

⊖ Electrical dual outlet

3. Students getting up to retrieve materials may disrupt students between them and the aisle.

Another design layout suited to direct instruction is the traditional column design (See Figure 4.2). Instead of the rows presented in the previous layout, the computers are arranged in columns from the front of the classroom stretching towards the rear of the room. The columns can generally be arranged back to back, so power and networking cabling can be run between the lines of desks with little problem. This design allows for good use of space, and it is a good layout for long narrow lab spaces. There are advantages to such a layout.

1. Good lines of sight for students in lecture, though some students will need to turn around to see the teacher.

2. Wiring is simple if the columns are against the rear wall, though this limits the ability of the teacher to move easily through the lab.

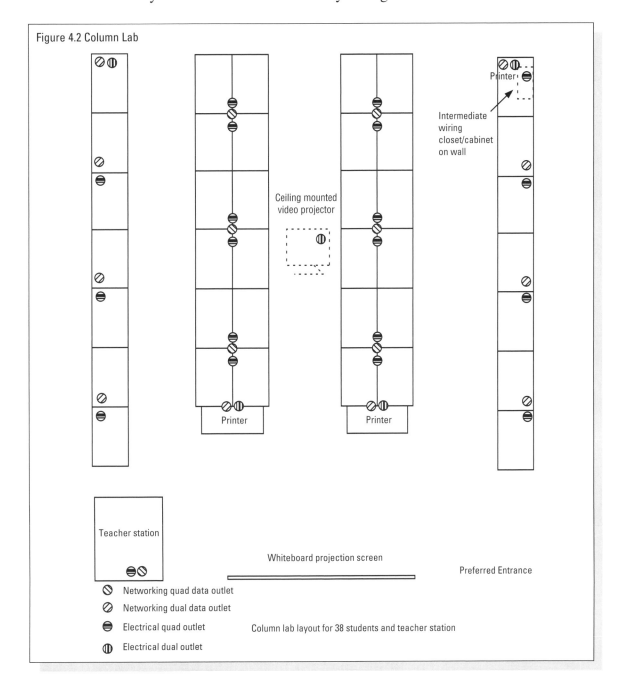

Figure 4.2 Column Lab

Printer

Intermediate wiring closet/cabinet on wall

Ceiling mounted video projector

Printer

Printer

Teacher station

Whiteboard projection screen

Preferred Entrance

⊘ Networking quad data outlet

⊘ Networking dual data outlet

⊖ Electrical quad outlet

⊕ Electrical dual outlet

Column lab layout for 38 students and teacher station

3. Furniture to support this layout is easy to obtain.

4. Students can move about without interrupting other students.

There are also disadvantages to the traditional column layout.

1. Student collaboration or group work is difficult.

2. The teacher cannot easily see all of the screens at any one time.

3. Students may not be able to see their screen and the teacher at the same time.

4. Some students may actually end up behind the teacher during most of a presentation.

The last of the designs suited for direct instruction is the horseshoe. The horseshoe lays out the computer stations in a horseshoe shape, with the open end facing the teaching station. The students sit around the outside of the horseshoe and all face in towards the center. There are advantages to such a layout.

1. Good lines of sight for the students to see the teacher, the board, or a projected image and their computer screen.

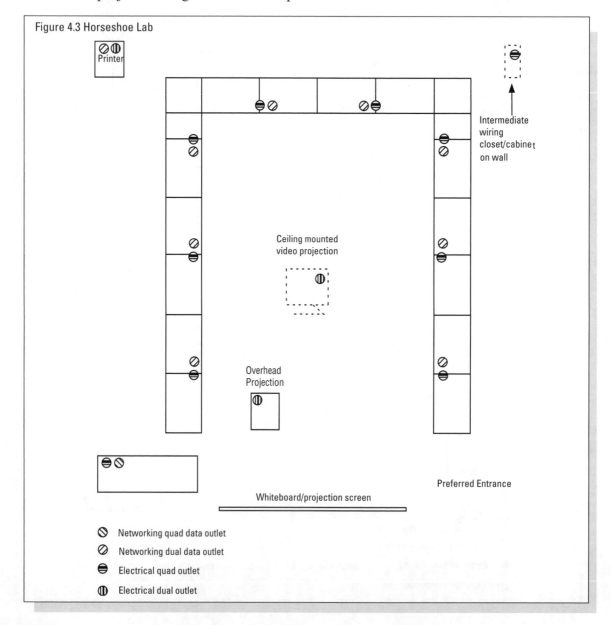

Figure 4.3 Horseshoe Lab

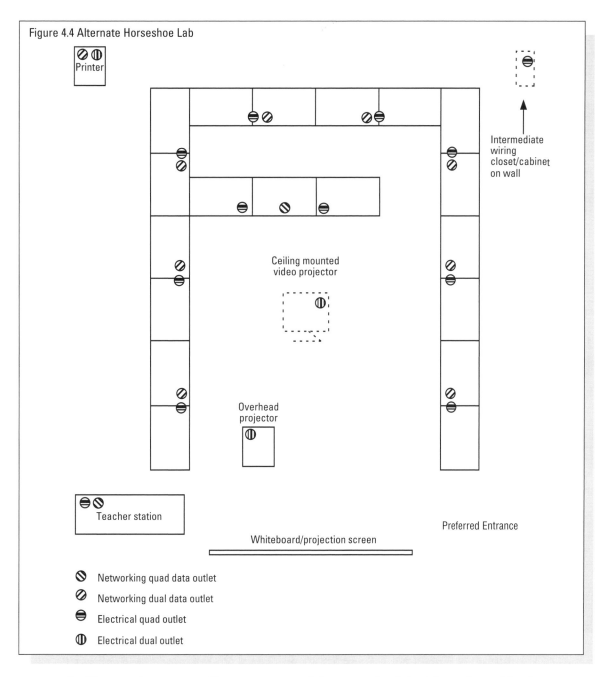

Figure 4.4 Alternate Horseshoe Lab

Printer

Intermediate wiring closet/cabinet on wall

Ceiling mounted video projector

Overhead projector

Teacher station

Preferred Entrance

Whiteboard/projection screen

Networking quad data outlet

Networking dual data outlet

Electrical quad outlet

Electrical dual outlet

2. The teacher can easily move around the room both inside and outside the horseshoe.

3. Power and data wiring can be run fairly easily around the inside of the horseshoe.

4. Students can easily enter and leave the lab without disrupting other students or the instructor.

5. Additional stations can be added in the center of the horseshoe for future expansion.

There are also disadvantages to the horseshoe layout.

1. Not designed for student collaboration or group work, though this design does allow for some collaboration.

2. The teacher cannot see all of the screens at any one time.

3. This design does not use space efficiently.

In many cases, the primary focus of a computer lab adjacent to the library media center is primarily for individual or small group production work. In situations where direct instruction is not a concern, a couple of other layouts are possible. The first of these is a wall-based layout (See Figures 4.5 and 4.6). In this situation, the computer stations are laid out along the outer perimeter of the room. This allows for easy access to each station for both students and the library media staff. In addition, other resources such as printers, scanners, or worktables can be put in the center. There are advantages to such a layout.

1. Easy supervision of all the stations.
2. Wiring for data and electricity can be based along the walls.
3. Good use of wall space.
4. Students have excellent access to all stations.

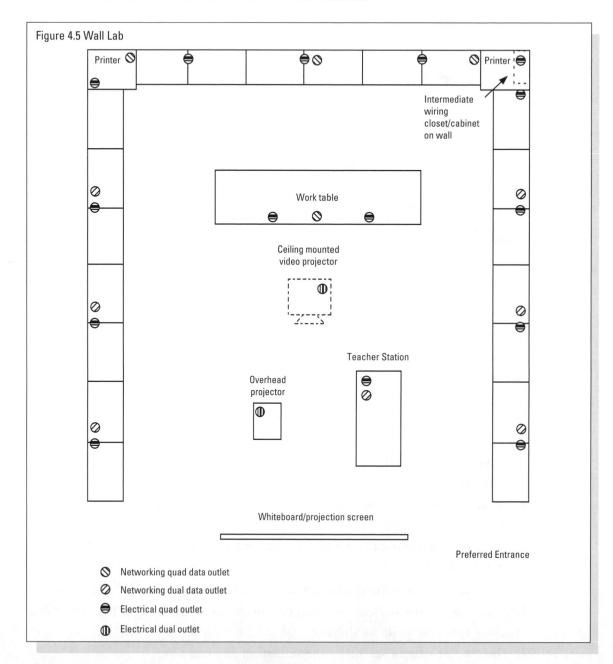

Figure 4.5 Wall Lab

Printer

Intermediate wiring closet/cabinet on wall

Work table

Ceiling mounted video projector

Teacher Station

Overhead projector

Whiteboard/projection screen

Preferred Entrance

⊘ Networking quad data outlet
⊘ Networking dual data outlet
⊜ Electrical quad outlet
⓪ Electrical dual outlet

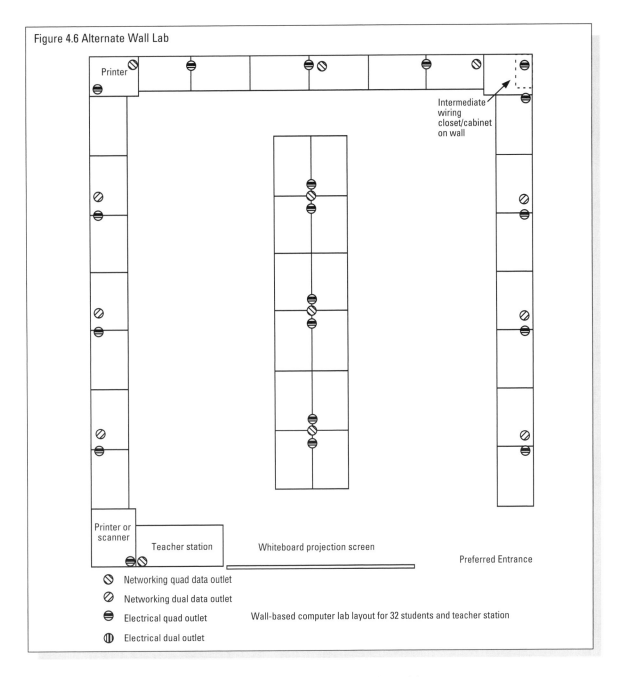

Figure 4.6 Alternate Wall Lab

Intermediate wiring closet/cabinet on wall

Printer

Printer or scanner

Teacher station

Whiteboard projection screen

Preferred Entrance

⊘ Networking quad data outlet

⊘ Networking dual data outlet

⊖ Electrical quad outlet   Wall-based computer lab layout for 32 students and teacher station

⦿ Electrical dual outlet

There are also disadvantages to the wall based layout.

1. Students would have to turn around to see an instructor.

2. Interior space is not well used.

3. Student collaboration is not fostered by this layout.

The island or pod layout (Figure 4.7) has been popular in many school settings, though it has a number of significant disadvantages. In this layout, the computers are placed throughout the space in groups of four to six machines. Usually, these layouts use specially-shaped hexagonal tables or contain several trapezoidal tables. There are advantages to such a layout.

1. Helps to facilitate cooperative work between students at each pod.

2. Easy for a teacher or student to move through the space.

3. Good space utilization in conjunction with the wall-based layout.

There are also disadvantages to the island or pod layout.

1. Some students would have to turn around to see an instructor.
2. The teacher cannot see all of the screens at once.
3. Wiring to each pod must be brought up through the floor or down from the ceiling.

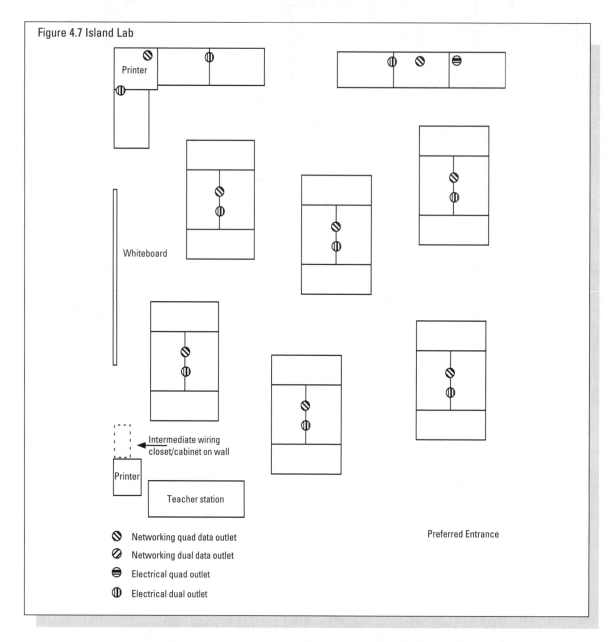

Figure 4.7 Island Lab

A layout that can facilitate collaboration between students and direct instruction is the repeated L. By arranging the stations in two or more lines of L's along the walls or out from the center, the students can easily work in either groups of two or four, yet all students can see the front of the room and the teacher. The teacher can also see all of the screens when she is standing in the rear of the lab. There are advantages to such a layout.

1. Easily supervise all stations.
2. Fosters student collaboration.

3. Students can all see both the teacher and their screen with little movement.

4. Wiring is fairly simple if the L's are wall based.

5. Students and teachers can access each station with little trouble.

Though the layout has many advantages, it is not always the most efficient use of space. It is better suited to square spaces than long narrow rooms.

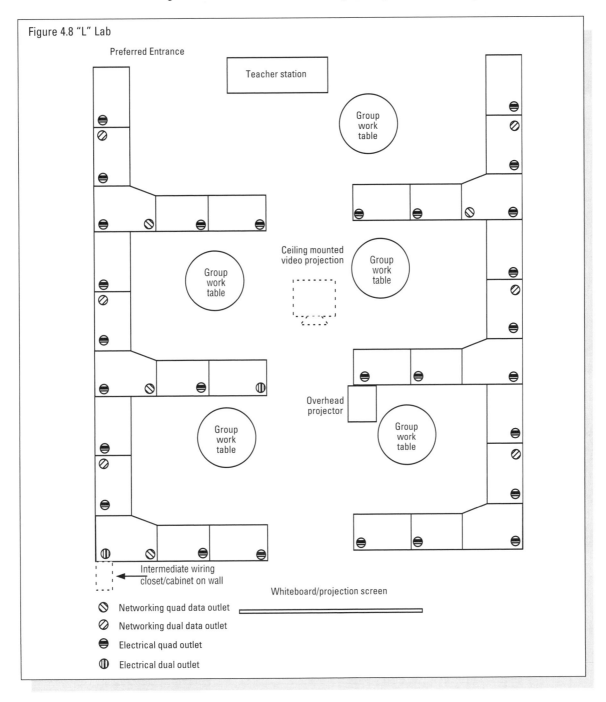

Figure 4.8 "L" Lab

Another lab layout that is becoming particularly popular is the tiered computer lab. Figures 4.9 and 4.10 are samples of tiered designs. Many new buildings are being built with tiered labs. These labs facilitate supervision because the teacher can see all of the computer screens at once from the front of the room.

In addition, many of these labs include a writing surface behind the student stations on each tier. These surfaces allow the teacher to keep students focused on the instructor as the students are turned away from their computers. (Anyone who has worked with students – or adults – in computer labs knows that many students play with the mouse or keyboard simply because it is in front of them.)

There are several advantages to such a layout:

1. Easily supervise all stations.
2. Students can easily see the teacher for instruction.
3. Wiring is fairly simple and can be brought up from underneath the tiers.
4. Space is well utilized.
5. Some variations of this layout naturally generate cooperative groupings.

There are several disadvantages of a tiered layout as well:

1. It requires two presentation systems, so that students can view presentations while working on the computer or the writing surface.
2. When students are working at their computers, their backs are to the instructor.
3. Tiers are difficult to modify, so future flexibility is limited.

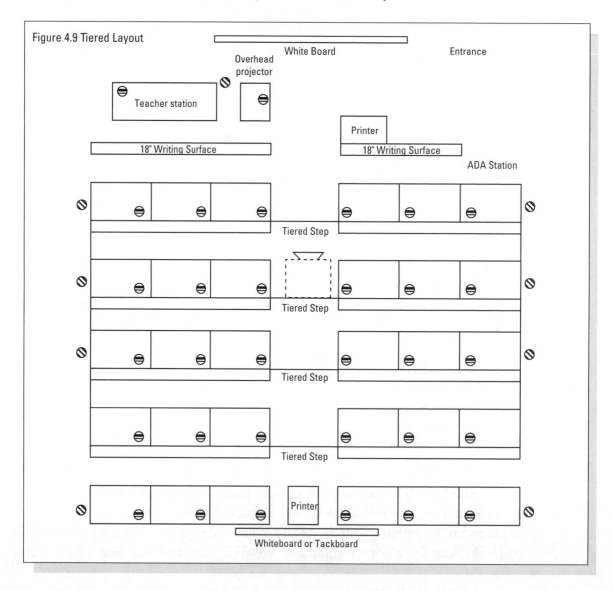

Figure 4.9 Tiered Layout

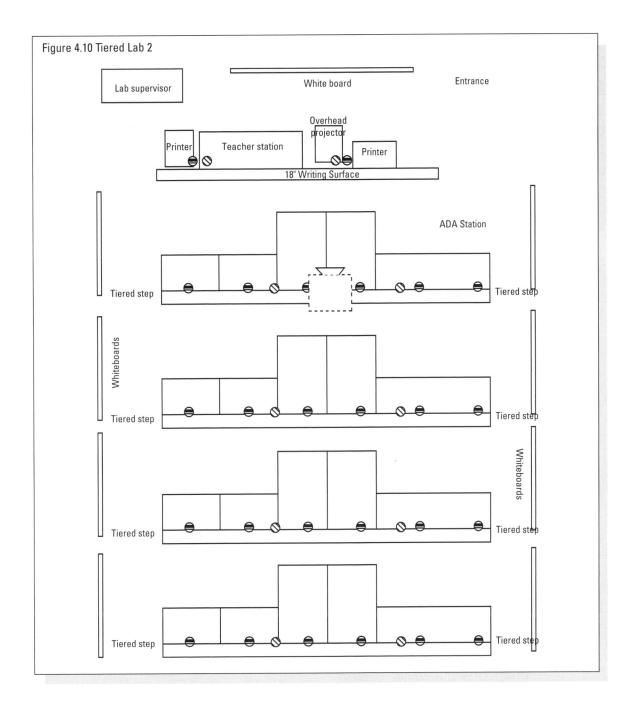

Figure 4.10 Tiered Lab 2

When building tiers for a lab, there are two guidelines to keep in mind. First, tiers should generally be six to 10 inches apart in height. This will allow for a gradual step increase and cause the fewest presentation disruptions. A gentle gradual rise is also important if the teacher is going to be going up and down the tiers all day. Second, long-term flexibility is important. In many cases, poured concrete tiers may appear to be the simplest solution, but poured concrete cannot be adapted to changing wiring or electrical needs. In contrast, when building a steel framework and pouring a thin concrete slab over it, one will have a strong infrastructure and still be able to move wiring and other equipment under the tiers. If, in the long term, changing instructional needs require the removal of the tiers, such a structure will be much easier to remove than solid concrete.

Presentation Issues in a Computer Lab

Presentation equipment will greatly enhance the instructional power of the computer lab. In nearly all of the examples shown, for instance, a video projector has been mounted in the lab ceiling. Modern video projectors allow for an extremely crisp image to be displayed, even in conditions of moderate to full light. When one compares the cost of video projectors to television monitors, video projectors are worth the additional cost.

When installing a video projector, wire the projector directly into the teaching station. Wire another input to a traditional video outlet, so the video projector can also be used to project a video or DVD. This outlet should be as close as possible to the teacher's station. Most video projectors come with a remote but some also include a wireless mouse that allows the instructor to move through computer presentations without being located at the teacher's station.

Another presentation option for a computer lab is a computerized white board. These boards have special pens that are used as a mouse directly on a white board where a screen image is being presented. In some cases, the white board can capture the text and diagrams an instructor writes on the board as computer files. These files can be saved for future lectures or sent to students who were absent.

A traditional overhead projector is also an advisable addition to any computer lab. Especially in mathematics courses, the traditional overhead is still an important tool and should not be overlooked.

Computer Supervisory Systems

In the last decade or so, a number of "remote control" supervisory systems have entered the educational marketplace. These systems generally come in two flavors: hardware systems and software systems. The hardware systems generally allow the instructor to take control of the student keyboards and mice. They can either manipulate student machines or simply prohibit the students from entering anything themselves. Hardware systems tend to be more expensive than the software based options.

The software-based systems tend to be an extension of security software programs. These systems allow instructors to see all of the students' screens on their monitor. Many of them allow the teacher to take control of the student computers and project the instructor's computer image onto the student screen. They can also prevent students from launching certain programs while the instructor is presenting to the class.

The advantages of these systems are:

- They can allow the instructor to view what the students are doing without the students knowing they are being watched.
- They can allow the instructor to control all of the computers.

These systems also have disadvantages:

- They tend to be expensive and software systems tend to take up large amounts of network bandwidth.

- They tend to lock the teacher into sitting at his computers in order to manage the system.
- The hardware systems tend to be specific to the equipment they were originally purchased for. Upgrading the lab equipment may make the systems unusable in the future.

Setting Up a Mobile Laptop Lab

In some cases, a dedicated space cannot be provided for a computer lab. In these cases, a mobile lab may be a reasonable solution. A mobile computer lab is similar to a regular computer lab except that is does not have its own space; it must be transported from room to room. Though these labs have been in use for several years, advances in wireless networking make them a more realistic option than in the past.

In setting up such a lab, the first thing to determine is how many computers will be needed. As with a traditional computer lab, the team will want to have extra machines on hand. Remember that laptop computers are more fragile than desktops and will need more maintenance than their desktop cousins.

After determining the number of computers needed, obtain one or two carts to move the computers through the school, thus making the lab mobile. Some commercial carts are motorized and even have batteries to recharge the laptops. However, even if the cart is electrified and contains a battery charger, one will still need to plug it in at the end of the day. Such carts allow the laptops to be recharged while in storage, which is easier than remembering to plug in each laptop every day. In addition, an electrified cart can connect the laptops to a printer on the cart or to the building LAN.

Laptop labs are expensive, but they are essential if the school cannot dedicate space to a traditional lab. However, do not forget that it will need a lab manager or teacher aide to support it. The lab will need to be supported, just like a traditional lab, especially if it is to be moved around the building during the day and connected and unconnected to the building LAN.

There are several advantages to a mobile lab:

1. The computers can be used in conjunction with other resources available in the classroom or library media center.
2. Teachers do not need to leave their regular classroom to use computers nor do they have to pack up their materials to move between rooms.
3. Students will not have to remember to go to the computer lab, nor is instructional time wasted going between the lab and the classroom.
4. No dedicated space is required, except to store the equipment.

There are also several disadvantages to a mobile lab:

1. The cost of a laptop tends to be 150 percent to 200 percent the cost of a similar desktop computer. Also, laptops are more fragile than desktop computers.

2. Laptop batteries are not yet able to go more than three or four hours without recharging. Therefore, they cannot provide a full day of use without being recharged.

3. Moving the laptops around the school requires staff commitment in most cases.

4. If the laptops are not plugged in at the end of the day, they may not be usable the next day.

5. Laptops do not facilitate the use of scanners or other peripherals, so these devices must be located in the media center or another computer lab.

6. The ergonomics of laptops tends to make them less than desirable for tasks lasting longer than a few minutes.

Figure 4.11 Laptop Cart 1

Figures 4.11, 4.12, are 4.13 provide some samples of laptop carts currently used in schools.

Besides the general layout of the computer stations themselves, there are several other items to consider when designing a computer lab. Any lab that will be used for direct instruction must include some method of video projection. Storage is also an important item to be addressed. Ensure that the layout provides storage for adequate amounts of paper and printer toner supplies, as well as software. Software and manuals should be kept in locked cabinets. The software can be kept in storage cabinets along the upper walls of the facility. Open storage directly above the computer stations can be used to store manuals or textbooks that the students will use regularly. Consider how to provide space for student books and backpacks. In some labs, the team will need to provide space for a wiring closet or IDF (Intermediate Distribution Facility or Frame) if the wiring terminates locally. Many labs will want to have a local server, and this will require a secure space.

Figure 4.12 Laptop Cart 2

Figure 4.13 Laptop Cart 3

The design team should also plan space for a lab supervisor, even if the position has not yet been created. This space should include the following:

- a desk with locking drawers
- a computer
- a phone
- locking file space either as part of the desk or within a separate cabinet
- workspace to collaborate with a teacher or assist a student.

Include a space for teachers to put their materials. A small counter or desk at the front of the lab will help teachers collect assignments or distribute handouts. Because the equipment in the computer lab is valuable, ensure that some type of security system is put in place to protect the investment.

Computer Furniture

Furniture requirements for computer labs are unique from most other spaces in a school. Lab furniture is specified in several ways. Traditional computer furniture or carts can be used. Cabinetry or millwork can be built specifically to meet the team's specifications. The design team can also specify traditional tables. The latter choice is not wise unless cost is a major consideration. Generally, regular tables or even recycled furniture from old typing labs is not built to handle computer equipment. One of the most significant limitations of furniture not specifically designed for computer use is a lack of wire management. When wires are not bundled and managed properly, they end up tangled in students' feet and chair legs. Sometimes chairs tangled around wiring bring computers to a crashing halt. If all the wiring will be kept against walls, such furniture is an option.

Traditional computer furniture tends to accommodate wire management, electrical needs, and the necessary pathways for keyboard and monitor wires. In general, such furniture also tends to be better designed for human ergonomics. The down side of computer furniture is that is tends to be boxy and built for a certain type of computer (desktop, mini-tower, 17-inch monitor). It also tends to be expensive. Many of the technical furniture lines are modular and allow a fair range of flexibility. A trend in this type of furniture is to eliminate many of the sharp edges and create softer more flowing edges by using curvilinear edges that provide better ergonomics for users.

Ergonomics

Ergonomic recommendations also include providing a range of furniture sizes so students can self-select the best size chair or table for their needs. Monitor heights should be set so that a student's eye level is two or three inches below the top of the screen. Monitors should always be adjustable in height and angle. Chairs should be adjustable and include adjustable armrests. Elbows should be between 90 and 100 degrees while typing. Students should be able to keep their wrists straight. Ergonomic experts suggest having students connect laptops to external keyboards and mice when possible, which is unrealistic in most instructional settings.

Figure 4.14 PC Mounted Below Table

Figure 4.15 Numbered Carrels

Another trend for computer labs is to select furniture that allows the computer equipment to be kept below the work surface. This type of furniture is becoming more popular in business settings. See Figure 4.14. It has both advantages and disadvantages in a lab setting. The advantages include:

- Eliminates obstacles to lines of sight between both teacher and students and among students.
- Provides additional table space at each user station
- Keeps most of the monitor and computer knobs and switches out of reach

The disadvantages include:

- Difficult to service.
- Difficult to see all of the student screens at once or in passing.
- Handprints and marks on the workstation surface hinder viewing of the monitor.
- The furniture may not easily handle changes in the shapes or sizes of technology.

A third alternative for furniture is to have a local cabinet maker or millwork shop create customized furniture. This can be a fairly inexpensive solution, and the planners will get exactly what they want. Have the cabinetmakers come in and discuss needs. Then ask them to return shop drawings for review. In many cases, the team will be surprised that the cost will be comparable to the other options. The disadvantage is that such customized furniture cannot be easily moved or modified.

In order to better identify lab stations, some schools number each workstation so teachers and other adults can easily identify which student is having problems or needs assistance. See Figure 4.15.

A Note on Language Labs

Figure 4.16 Language Carrels

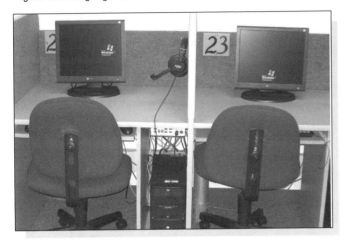

In the past, most foreign language labs have been fairly tightly packed with student carrels. As technology changes and traditional analog (audiotape) labs are worn out, they will need to be replaced with labs for both analog media and computer-based digital technologies. This will require additional space in two areas. The student carrel dimensions must be expanded to allow the inclusion of a computer and monitor. Since students will likely need more assistance with computers than when they only had to turn a tape recorder on or off, better access for teachers to each station will be necessary.

If the design project includes installing a language lab, consider a computer lab layout that allows good direct instruction. However, because most student collaboration in language labs is fostered by the audio components of the system, a layout that facilitates interaction between students may not be desirable. See Figure 4.16.

No matter what type of computer resources the design team needs to accommodate, careful consideration needs to be given to computer spaces. Like the library media center itself, computer labs are high traffic areas that will be used by every student in the building. Ensure the design team carefully considers the advantages and disadvantages of each layout option before making a final decision.

Chapter 5

Sample Media Center Layouts

The following pages offer possible library media center designs. In most of the samples, all possible areas are not included. Priorities and space allotments usually limit the amount and kinds of spaces that the center will be able to include. Though the designs are labeled as elementary, middle school, and high school, most of the designs could be modified for any type of school depending upon the space available. A few general comments have been included for each sample design.

Elementary Library Media Center Layout #1:

The design in Figure 5.1 would be a good starting point for a small elementary school with a single library media specialist. The computer lab is included as an integral part of the library media center. A fair amount of seating is provided, along with a raised story area in the corner. A possible outside entrance could allow the library media center to be kept open in the evening or during the summer without having to open up the rest of the school.

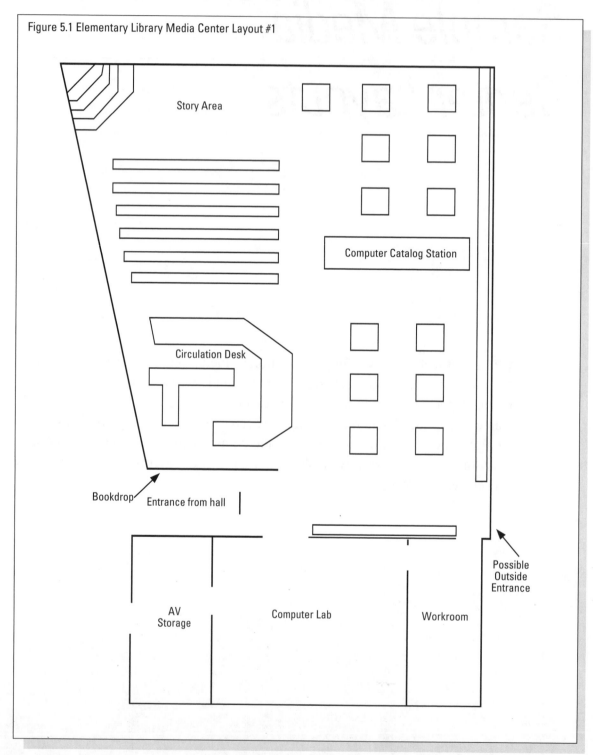

Figure 5.1 Elementary Library Media Center Layout #1

Elementary Library Media Center Layout #2:

The design in Figure 5.2 allows the media center to have a main entrance near the school's main entrance, but also provides easy access for teachers from the classroom wing of the building. The student production area is separate from the computer lab, but a computer lab could easily be attached to the media center on either side. The circulation desk allows good supervision of the entire media center.

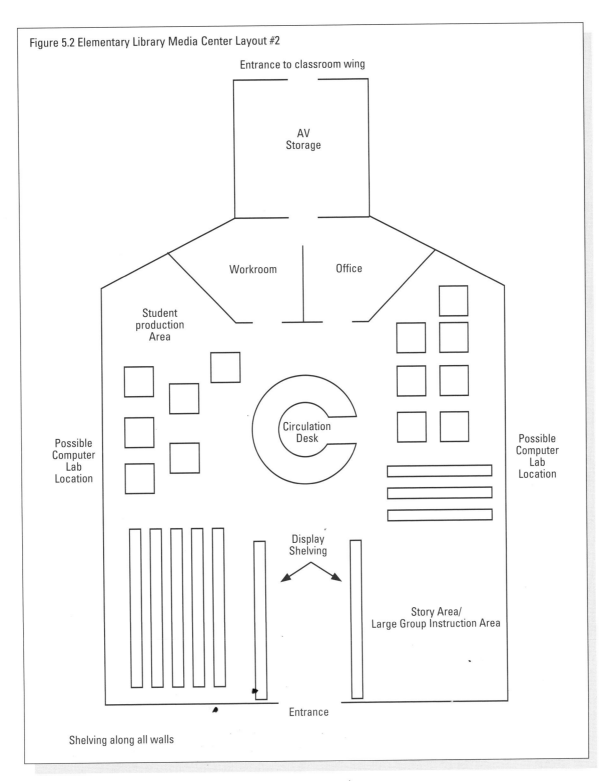

Figure 5.2 Elementary Library Media Center Layout #2

Elementary Library Media Center Layout #3:

The layout in Figure 5.3 is intended to fit within the confines of two regular classrooms. The circulation desk, as this design shows, does not have to be a large edifice in the middle of the library media center. Easy access to a computer lab and access to an outside entrance are accomplished in this design. As in the other elementary designs, a single staff member will operate the media center.

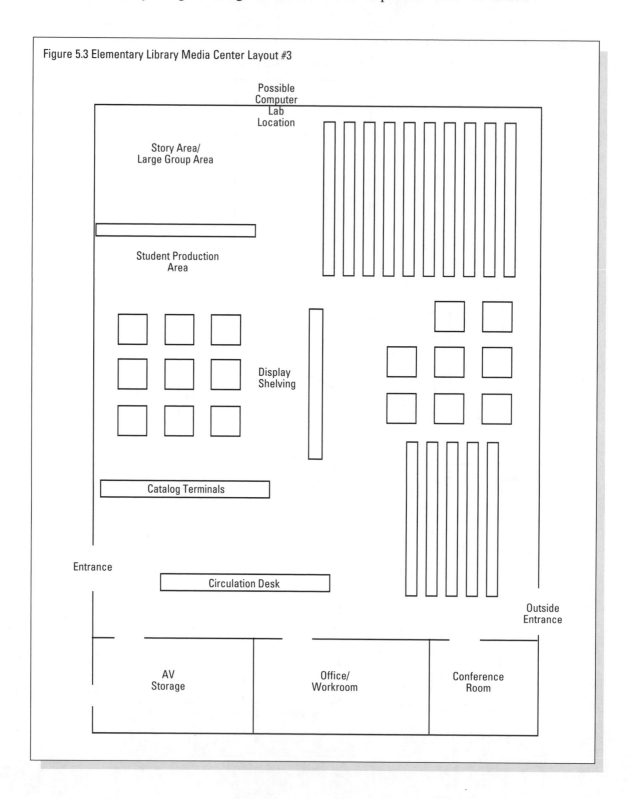

Figure 5.3 Elementary Library Media Center Layout #3

Middle School Library Media Center Layout #1:

Figure 5.4 shows a layout that allows for three classes to be in the media center simultaneously. This design includes a large computer reference and production area. The circulation desk is placed to allow supervision of all areas except for the large group area. A small amount of comfortable seating or a quiet study area is included next to the circulation desk. The far end of the library media center has conference rooms and a large group or team area. These areas help address the needs of multiple instructional groups becoming common in most middle schools and many high schools. This design features a separate audio-visual service desk, a large audio-visual storage and repair facility, and a darkroom.

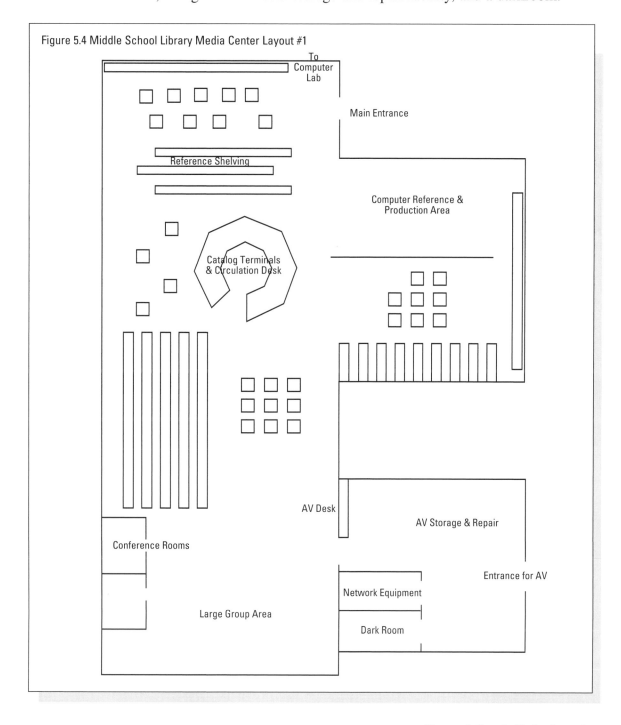

Figure 5.4 Middle School Library Media Center Layout #1

Middle School Library Media Center Layout #2:

The design in Figure 5.5 offers a smaller amount of seating space than the previous design, but includes a significant amount of computer production space. The large group area is separated from the rest of the library media center by a wall, which supports a raised seating area. This space allows easy control of lighting for computer or video projection, book talks, and storytelling. This design assumes that a lab supervisor in the computer area will be able to help with supervision of the far end (the end away from the entrance) of the media center.

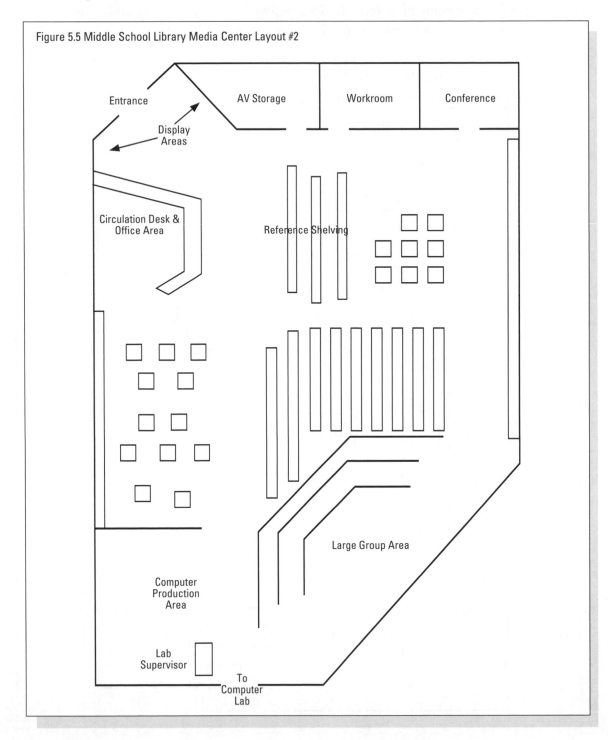

Figure 5.5 Middle School Library Media Center Layout #2

High School Library Media Center Layout #1:

Figure 5.6 shows a design intended for a large high school with two or more library media specialists and several support staff. It includes seating for four classes, plus additional seating in the reference area for computer users. The computers in this media center are divided into two groups. Near the entrance are computers to be used primarily for research. At the far end of the library media center is a computer lab for general productivity. This design supports 80 computers for student use. The design includes a technical services area where district cataloging and processing could be conducted.

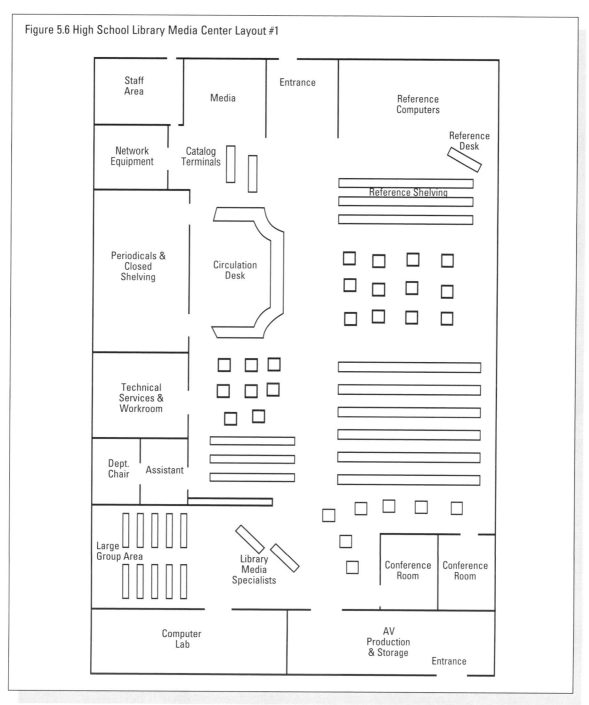

Figure 5.6 High School Library Media Center Layout #1

High School Library Media Center Layout #2:

Simple supervision with minimal staffing is key to the design in Figure 5.7. A computer lab and other audio-visual equipment take up a large amount of the floor space. Conference rooms can be combined by folding up the partition between the rooms. The computer lab provides easy access to the library's faculty workroom. The computer lab can be entered without opening the rest of the library media center. With proper placement in the building, the main entrance can allow access from the outside through the same hallway. The large group area in the corner could be designed to be a computer lab.

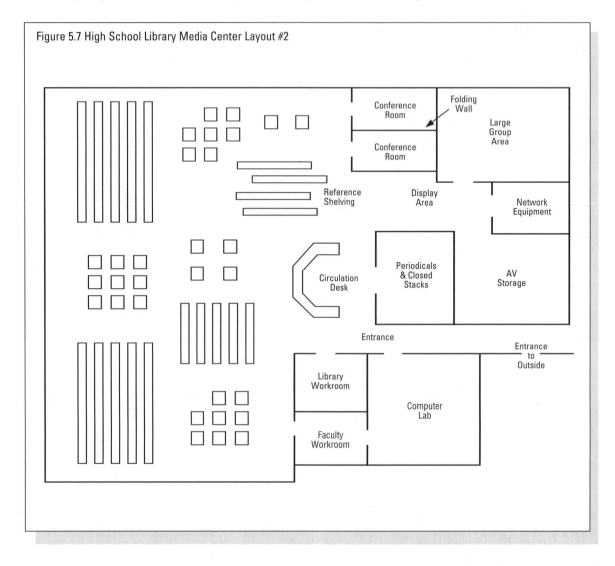

Figure 5.7 High School Library Media Center Layout #2

High School Library Media Center Layout #3:

The layout in Figure 5.8 is for a high school with two or more library media specialists plus support staff. The design includes three classroom seating areas, plus a large group or quiet study area. A fair amount of conference space is available. Mobile walls provide flexible space within the conference rooms. The computer lab is divided into two areas. One can be used primarily for productivity work, while the other lab should be equipped for multimedia development. A significant display area is included near the entrance. The shelving can be angled to allow better supervision from the circulation desk. Unlike the first high school sample, this design provides off the floor office space for the library media specialists.

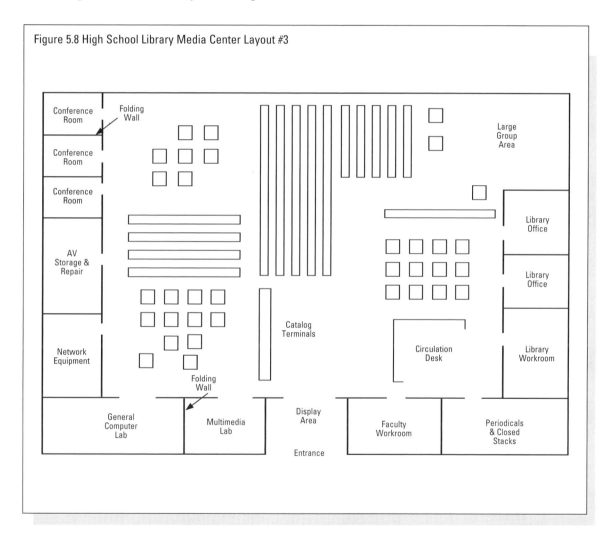

Figure 5.8 High School Library Media Center Layout #3

High School Library Media Center Layout #4:

In Figures 5.9a and 5.9b the design is on a two-floor layout. Although not a preferred design, sometimes space requirements will dictate a two-floor arrangement. This design allows for several class spaces and an integrated technology program. A general computer lab, with a separate entrance from an upper floor hallway, is near a smaller multimedia lab. A staff development lab is located on the lower level. The circulation and reference desks are designed to allow some supervision from the lower level of the upper level.

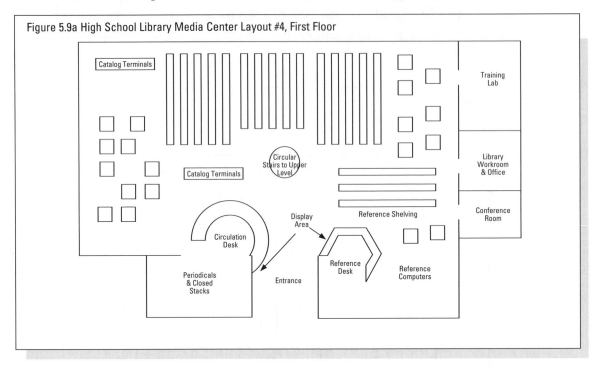

Figure 5.9a High School Library Media Center Layout #4, First Floor

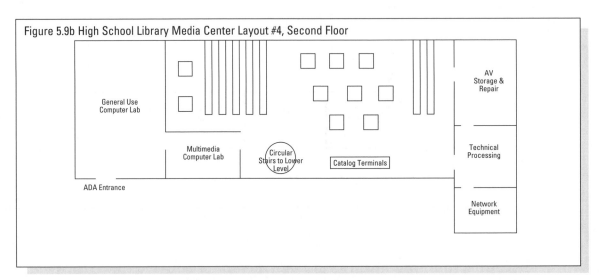

Figure 5.9b High School Library Media Center Layout #4, Second Floor

The designs here are only a starting point. They are representative of many existing library media centers. In determining layouts, the design team should review this chapter, visit other local library media centers, local public libraries, search for floor plans posted on the Internet, and ask the architectural firm to provide examples of its past work.

Chapter 6

Creating Bids and Timelines

Once the design team has determined needs, articulated the size, type, and number of tables needed, agreed on the number of computers, and come to conclusion on where video projectors should be mounted, the team must take that information and distill it into a form that the architect, trades people, and vendors can understand. These final documents are known as bid specifications. They provide a systematic way to allow a wide range of vendors to bid on the team's project. A competitive bid process should allow the school or district to obtain the greatest value for the least cost. This is why most public schools can not simply go to their favorite vendor and order items that are above a certain dollar amount. Being stewards of public funds requires a bid process for most projects. Most private schools also bid larger projects as the competitive bid process can save a school considerable money.

RFP's or Bid Documents

One important aspect of the facilities design process is the development of good competitive bid specifications (bid specs) or a well-defined request for proposal (RFP). In all cases, the facilities design team should not expect to develop the bid requirements without assistance from the business manager and possibly an outside consultant as well. It is critical from a legal standpoint that the bid specifications allow all bidders to be judged on equal terms.

Bid specifications are developed for two important purposes. The first purpose is to specify the specific equipment, materials, or services required including warranties, and training to be provided. The second purpose of the bid specifications is to determine if the bidder is capable and qualified to provide the equipment, material, or services requested.

The bid documents must itemize each item to be provided. This can be done in two ways. One method is to describe a standard that the equipment must meet. As an example, the specs would specify a desktop computer with a 3.4 GHz Pentium processor that has 256MB of RAM, a 8.4 GB or larger hard drive, and a 15 inch or larger monitor.

The second method would be to specify a proprietary item. This method specifies the item by brand name, model number, and more. Using the same computer example, the specs would specify a Dell XPS 800. Many schools and government agencies prefer to provide descriptive standards, because they feel the development of bid specifications based upon brand name items is unfair. Development along proprietary lines is a simple way to develop a bid specification, and as long as multiple suppliers can furnish the brand requested, the bid process is not compromised.

Once standards have been set, they can be modified to some extent. In some cases, the specifications should be "closed." That means only the exact product requested in the specifications is provided. No substitutions are allowed. In some cases, the specs can allow multiple options for the bidder to choose from. Any product from the designated list would be acceptable. In other cases, the design team may want to allow "or equivalent," which would leave the bidder the option to provide an alternative item meeting the same standards as the items specified. Allowing equivalent items is usually not a good idea in bidding technology-related items because many alternatives are normally available and judging the multiple facets of an alternative against the specified item is often impossible. The equivalent becomes a problem in judging all bids on a level playing field. In general, however, allow for a newer generation of the same product to be bid without penalty. For instance, if the bid specified a 3.2 GHz processor, but the vendor chose to propose a 4.2 GHz processor, do not penalize the vendor.

In other areas, such as furniture, the use of equivalent items is often a benefit as a bidder may find an identical item that can provide the exact same performance from another vendor at a lower price. In some cases, the school administration can require that any alternate submitted requires prior approval in order to be included with the bid. Requiring submission of an alternative prior to bidding allows one to determine whether or not the team would be happy with any alternative provided on an item-by-item basis. The bid specifications should include the level and length of warranty to be provided by the bidder. Specific installation and shipping dates may also be outlined in the bid specs but usually need to be somewhat flexible depending upon the size of the project.

Bidders should provide both a unit price for each item and the total extension for each line of the bid. This assists the team and the business office in determining the successful bid proposal in a timely manner. Request a unit price for any additional number of the item that the team decides to purchase. For instance, the original order contains 35 chairs, figuring that the school will not be able to afford all 50 that the team really needs. When the bids come in, the price is so low that the school can now afford to purchase the additional chairs. If the bidder has already had to specify the cost of any additional chairs, one does not have to negotiate the additional cost. The school can simply order 50 not 35 at the competitive price that has already been determined. The bid spec should specify that the installation and delivery are included within the bid for each group of items. If the school is on a narrow side street or is an old building with a narrow loading dock or no elevator, the maximum size of the delivery truck may need to be specified. If the school is a tax-exempt institution, the bidders should be instructed not to include taxes within their quotes.

The second section of the bid specification should ask for enough information about the vendor to determine whether or not the bidder will be able to complete the work and deliver the equipment specified. In this section the specs should ask if the vendor is an authorized reseller or partner qualified to sell the equipment specified. Any bidder must be an authorized reseller for any equipment quoted. Bidders who are not authorized resellers should be automatically disqualified. In the same manner, when bidding large projects, the bidder should have to provide some general financial information, the length of time they have been in business, their ability to service the products requested, the amount of qualified installers, and the number of service people on staff.

Generally, a bidder may need to comply with one or more of the following:
- Provide bid bonds or completion bonds.
- Provide payrolls that match prevailing wage scales for the local area.
- Provide proof of liability insurance or similar bonds.
- Provide proof of manufacturer or state certification.
- Attend mandatory pre-bid and pre-construction meetings.

Bidding Wiring or Electrical Work

For wiring or electrical work, the specs will need to determine what type of certifications or union affiliations the bidder has. Ask for a number of references based upon work done in a similar (school or library) setting and by the same project manager. In some cases, the vendor will provide references for a project team that is not the one assigned to do the work at the location. Ensure that at least two or three of the references provided are for the *specific project manager* who will be assigned to the project. Retain the right to reject a bidder based upon poor references. For large projects, develop a pre-qualification procedure to eliminate any bidders without enough experience, staff, or positive references to properly complete the project being bid. In many states, the vendors also need to identify their support of a drug-free workplace, pay prevailing wages (wages based upon union pay scales), and comply with other state or federal regulations.

Pre-Bid Walkthrough

Bids that consist of any level of construction or onsite installation require a *pre-bid walkthrough or survey*. In this situation, all of the vendors hoping to bid on the project come to the site where the work will be done, walk through the facility with the bid specifications, and ask any questions they may have about the project. Such a walkthrough helps to ensure that the bidders have a good understanding of the project and keeps all of the bids on an even playing field. Walkthroughs help to defuse later vendor complaints claiming they did not understand the whole scope of the project. During the walkthrough, someone from the school district should provide each potential bidder a running list of all questions and official responses. Sending the list of questions and answers to all participating vendors will help to keep the playing field level.

Contingency Funds

In cases where the scope of the project is large or variables exist in the final stages of the project, the school may want to include a set amount of contingency dollars (an owner's contingency) within the bid itself. Where the board of education requires that all projects come in within budget, such a contingency will help the project come in within budget, but at the same time it allows the room necessary to make the changes that will likely appear during the course of a large project.

Normally the owner's contingency should be set as a particular dollar amount so that all bidders will be on an equal playing field. At times this contingency is expressed as a percentage of the total project, but an exact dollar amount is easier to compare between bidders. In a large wiring project for instance, another few drops may be added as the project evolves. The owner's contingency will allow for those data drops to be added without going over budget.

Ensure that if equipment needs to be installed or work is to be done that the bid specifications state a definitive timeline as to when the work will be accomplished. As soon as the bid has been awarded, require the successful bidder to submit a comprehensive project timeline. Refer to it in the weekly construction meetings to determine whether or not the project is continuing on schedule. One may want to include a liquidated damages clause that requires the bidder to forfeit a certain amount of money for each day beyond the specified completion date that it takes to complete the project.

In cases where the project is moderate to large in scope, break the project bids into several groups. You may want to bid all of the basic furniture as one group, while the computer furniture is grouped separately. Such grouping allows the school to award the projects with more flexibility than if the project is awarded as a lump sum. However, awarding the bids to several vendors requires more coordination on the part of the school district. If the school awards the project in sections or groups, specify that the successful bidders attend weekly or bi-monthly coordination meetings during the course of the project to ensure the necessary coordination.

Timelines

The design and construction of educational spaces is a particularly time consuming task. In order to complete the process in a successful manner, begin planning more than a year in advance of the proposed opening date. When the board of education gives the go ahead for the renovation or building project, the planning process must begin in earnest. The first thing to do is to form the design team. At the same time as the design team is being formed, talk to several vendors informally to determine the amount of lead time necessary to deliver furniture or other equipment when an order is placed. In many cases, furniture delivery times can easily exceed 10 to 12 weeks. If the order is placed in the middle of the summer, when every other school is also ordering new furniture and equipment, delivery times can be extended even more. Knowing what these times are is important as the team starts to determine when the board of education accepts the bids to ensure the work is done on schedule. Knowledge of the lead times allows the backward planning process to be completed.

Backward Planning

"Backward planning" begins with determining the "grand opening" date. If that is August 15, 2010, work back to how long will be needed for media center staff to set up the media center. If it will take three weeks to restock the collection after all other work is done, note the date, July 24, 2010. This three-week period allows time to install circulation software on the necessary computers, shelve the books in the collection, organize the supplies ordered, and otherwise prepare for opening.

From this date, determine how long it should take to install the furniture and shelving when it is delivered. Note the date, July 1, 2010, and move backwards once more. Now determine when to order the furniture. In this case, the vendors explain they will need 10 weeks for delivery, so note April 15, 2010. Ask the business manager when the board meeting closest to that date is and how long a bid notice must be posted according to state and local requirements. If the closest board meeting will be April 2, 2010, and the bid notice needs to be posted for 10 days, the bids will have to be posted approximately March 20, 2010. However, that is during spring break, so add another week as a buffer. The bids will therefore be posted March 10, 2010, to allow enough time to examine the bids and recommend the winning bidders to the board.

If the team feels it will take approximately six weeks to develop the bid specifications, decisions about what to order must be made by January 15, 2010. If the architect wants three months to develop designs and floor plans and make modifications with the design team, that process should start no later than September 2009. Because the team wants to make site visits and take time to conduct their needs assessments, schedule two to three months to conduct the needs assessment, and the date needs to be moved back to March 2009.

As the summer months are difficult for communication with most school groups, do not count those months as time towards conducting activities with staff members. Before starting to plan the new facilities, visit several other sites and give the team at least two months to do that. This takes the timeline to January 2009. It may take a couple of weeks to gather the design team, which will take the schedule to November 2008.

Sample Timeline
■ Library media center grand opening: 8/15/2010
■ Final completion date for bidders: 7/24/2010
■ Arrival of furniture: 7/1/2010
■ Order for furniture placed: 4/15/2010
■ Bid notice for furniture placed: 3/10/2010
■ Construction bids awarded: 2/1/2010
■ Construction bid notice placed: 1/15/2010
■ Bid documents approved: 1/15/2010
■ Design team approved final design: 9/15/2009
■ Begin needs assessment: 3/1/2009
■ Begin facilities visits: 1/15/2009
■ Form planning team: 11/1/2008
■ Project approved by board: 10/1/2008

The entire design process will take nearly two years from the time the project is approved in concept by the board of education until the facility is opened. The best method is to simply keep a timeline and mark off items as they are added to the list and when they are completed. The team will need to specify the times necessary for the wiring consultants to do their design work, for the interior designer to work on color schemes and other things. Project management is an important task. Remember, if the first phases take too long or are not given enough time the staff and students will be the ones playing catch up in the end. The vendor is not going to shorten his delivery or installation time! That just will not happen nor is it reasonable to count on it.

Creating bid specifications or RFPs, if not going through a formal bid process, takes time and an eye for detail. The design team needs to have a number of visionary "big picture" types on the team to lead the needs assessment process. The team needs some detail-oriented members as well who can lead the development and review of the bid specs. This is an essential phase of the project because bid specs are how the team will communicate its wishes to the vendors who will do the work. One should not assume that the architects and business office staff will totally understand the team's desires. Throughout the process, the design team needs to be engaged in reviewing the development of the bid specs and reviewing the bids that are submitted.

Throughout this process it is essential to keep an eye on the calendar. Being a slave to the specified timeline and demanding the design team meets its deadlines will allow the vendors the time they need to complete your project on time. Nothing is better than opening a new media center on time. Few things are more frustrating than not being able to open the space because the shelving has not arrived or the computers have not been set up.

Chapter 7

Wrapping Up

Moving Out and Moving Back In

In the best-case scenario, the library media center the team is designing is a new library and there will be nothing to pack up and move. However, that is not normally the case. Even if the staff is moving into new construction, the staff may be moving out of an old media center and might have to take some, if not all, of the equipment and books to the new facilities. Consider a number of items when developing a plan for packing and unpacking the library media center.

One of the biggest issues will be packing up, storing, and later unpacking and reshelving the print collection. A number of options are available. The easiest and the most expensive is hiring a company to come in and pack up the library media center. There are companies that specialize in such work. Such companies will rent special book carts on rollers for book storage as another option.

However, the average school budget will require another course of action. The most practical option is to plan to pack up the collection with existing staff. First, determine how many boxes it will take to hold the collection. It is best to purchase some new boxes of a manageable size than to try to scrounge up boxes around the school. When finished, the school can sell the boxes to recoup some of the cost of new boxes. Start by boxing up a couple of shelves from different areas of the collection as a trial. Determine how long it takes to box the average shelf and then multiply out how long it will take to pack up the collection.

Weed the Collection

Because the moving process takes up a good deal of time and energy, "weed like a fiend" prior to even starting to plan for the packing up of the collection! Remember, if the book has not circulated in two years, odds are it never will. In renovating most media centers, rearranging the shelving will occur even if no expansion of shelving will occur. As the staff packs the collection, consider the new shelving arrangement. Pack up two-thirds of a present shelf for placement on a new shelf if the shelving is expanding. Otherwise, pack each shelf in its own box, which allows one to unpack the collection more quickly.

When one has determined how to pack up the collection, determine how to mark each box. One suggestion is to color code each section of the collection and then number each shelf's box in sequence. Mark more than one side of the box, because "Murphy's Law" ensures the boxes will be stacked so one cannot see all of the markings otherwise.

With periodicals, one may want to use smaller boxes, as they tend to be heavier than a similar volume of books. Pack software, videos, and other audiovisual media separately. Because AV boxes will generally be more fragile than book boxes, do not stack them underneath heavier book boxes. Determine a place to put books that are returned while the collection is packed up so they do not get lost in the shuffle.

The team must plan for a place to store the collection while the construction is underway. Stages or dance rooms are perfect storage spots. These spaces tend to be large, open spaces that are unused in the summer. Cafeterias are another option. Where possible, stack the collection up in the reverse of how it will be unpacked. Make sure whatever space is used for storage is secure and unused during the construction period. Also make sure that no construction work is being done in or above the storage space. If the roof above the space is going to be worked on over the summer, such a space is not a good choice. The storage area must be climate controlled. If the construction is taking place during the school year, off site storage will be necessary.

Store computer equipment securely while the construction goes on. Most technology equipment must be protected from moisture and the extreme summer heat of a locked room in a closed-up school. In many cases, it is easier to send the equipment home with staff members over the summer than storing it at school.

Each piece of equipment should be marked as to where it goes in the new layout. Coordinate with the technology staff to obtain any help disconnecting and moving the computer equipment. In some cases, all the mice and keyboards can be collected and boxed up.

Box the supplies in the reverse order of how they will be needed. Clearly mark each container as to what it contains. Keep the scissors, tape, markers, and other marking supplies out until the end. Have staff members pack up their own desks and mark all of their furniture and files as clearly belonging together.

Determine where furniture will be stored and any shelving or other furniture that will be put back into the renovated space. Furniture can normally be kept in the hallways during the summer. If the old furniture is not to return, make it available to the rest of the staff and then work with the custodial staff to dispose of any leftover furniture in advance of any new furniture being delivered. In disposing of furniture or other materials, ask the district what process to follow.

Unpacking

With everything well labeled, unpacking should be easy. Have the design team help unpack and tidy up the new space. Enlist temporary staffing or extra parent volunteers to assist in the unpacking and "getting the place up and running" phase of the process. Do not get discouraged; it always takes longer to get everything the way one wants it than anticipated. Keep in mind how much nicer the space is than the old library media center.

In the end, all of the work is worth it. Enjoy the new space. Now start to look around and plan where signage needs to go. That will be the team's last design step.

The Necessary Communications

Now the team must communicate the features of the new or renovated library media center to teachers, students, and the board and administration. Be sure to show thanks for all of the hard work the design team put into the planning process and the support the administration and board provided by funding the project. Use some of the new display space to showcase specific features of the library media center or use signs to point out new or special features. Use an easel with butcher paper or a Power Point presentation to showcase the new production services available for students and teachers. If new titles were added to the collection, display them prominently for students.

If the media center was renovated, arrange to give a brief orientation to all the classes during the first few weeks of school so that students will not miss expanded services that they were not used to in the past. If the media center is in a new school, arrange to make the library media center a part of the overall orientation of the new facility for the students.

In either case, take the time to create a brochure of the resources and services available through the library media program. The brochure should include media center hours, check out policies, and the non-print materials available for loan or use in the media center. It should list the software and kinds of hardware (scanners, color printers) available for use. Provide information on whom to contact when scheduling a class within the library media center and whom to call for help. List the library media center home page URL and the fax number in the brochure.

In some cases, it may be a good idea to produce two slightly different versions of the brochure. One version will be for teachers and another for students and parents. The student and parent version can be included in the before school welcoming packets for students, handed out at parent-teacher conferences, and back to school nights. Inform the teachers regularly of any changes in library media program services or resources at faculty meetings or in a media center newsletter.

Figure 7.1

For the first back-to-school night or parent-teacher conference evening after the media center is complete, provide punch and cookies or some other snack to lure the parents (and the teachers) into the library media center. During the first National Library Week or National Education Week after the media center has been completed, arrange for a short reception to get all of the teachers into the library media center for an informal gathering. Invite the school board, the district administration, local public librarians, and the library media specialists from other buildings in the district as well.

Plan to continue an ongoing public relations campaign to continually promote the services the library media program has to offer. At the end of the first year in the new space, provide the building principal and the original design team with a review of the library media program. Be sure to highlight the additional services for the students and teachers that are due to the new space and resources that were provided.

Summary

At this point, the design team should be ready to move forward on its design project. The text provides an overview of how to gather the planning team (Chapter One). Chapter Two guides the team through the development of a thorough needs assessment. Chapter Three articulates how to specify needs for the new media center. These needs include everything from computers, seating, and shelving to color, lighting, and data wiring. Computer labs, which are intimately tied to strong library media programs, are addressed in Chapter Four. Sample layouts for the media center are provided for the team to use as starting points for its own layout designs. Chapter Six addresses the development of bid specifications and timelines for projects. The last chapter provides general considerations on packing up existing spaces and moving into new ones.

From this point, the book includes a number of appendices with samples the design team can use to build custom programming documents, needs assessment surveys, and site visit questionnaires. A bibliography of additional resources and a listing of Web sites are also included to assist the design team in its work. A glossary is included to help in understanding the construction vernacular.

Good luck and happy designing!

Bibliography

AASL. (2002). *Knowledge Quest.* Books and Bricks Issue 31 (1).

AASL. (1998). Information Power: 1998 update. <http://www.ala.org/aasl>.

ALA & AECT. (1988). *Information Power: Guidelines for School Library Media Programs.* Chicago: ALA. (This edition includes more specifics about facilities than the newer edition.)

Baule, S. M. (1998). Media Centers Designed for Technology. *School Executive Supplement to Media and Methods* 34 (3): S-6.

Baule, S. M. (2005). Planning Considerations for Library Media Centers. *Library Media Connection* 45 (3): 14-15.

Bloch, M. (2006). High-Wireless Act: The Reality of Airborne School Connections. *Scholastic Administrator* 5 (4): 38-41.

Brown, C. R. (1995). *Planning Library Interiors: The Selection of Furnishing for the 21st Century.* Phoenix: Oryx Press.

Brown, C. R. (1989). *Selecting Library Furniture.* Phoenix: Oryx Press.

Buchanan, B. (1990). Drawing Strength. *School Library Journal* 36 (2): 21-25.

Dolan, T. G. (2004). Library or Media Center. *School Planning and Management* 43 (4). Available at <http://www.peterli.com/archive/spm/655.shtm>.

Enriquez, D. (1999). Let There Be Light! *Library Talk* 12 (5): 8-9.

Fanning/Howey Associates, Inc. (2001). *Facilities Design Perspectives: Community Use of Schools.* Celina, OH: Fanning/Howey.

Fanning/Howey Associates, Inc. (1998). *Middle Schools: Shaping the Future.* Celina, OH: Fanning/Howey.

Fitterman, L. J. (1998). Ergonomics: The Forgotten Variable. *Technology Connection* 5 (3): 7+.

Fraley, R. A. & Anderson, C. L. (1990). *Library Space Planning.* New York: Neal-Schuman.

Green Supplement. (2006). *School Planning & Management* 45 (4): G-1 - G-43.

Haggans, Michael. (1998). 14 Ways to Get Better Performance from Your Architect. *School Planning & Management* 37 (3): 24-27.

Hart, T. L. (2005). Library Media Facilities Access: Do You Really Want Your Library Media Center USED? *Library Media Connection* 24 (3): 16-19.

Hart, T. L. (2006). Top Ten List of Library Facility Technology Issues. *Library Media Connection* 24 (4): 46-47.

Hawkins, H.L. (1997). The Uncertain Future of High School Library Design. *School Planning & Management* 36 (10): 7.

Illinois Library Association. (1992). *Illinois School Library Media Program Guidelines.* Chicago: Illinois Library Association.

Illinois State Board of Education. (1986). *Recommended Standards for Educational Library Media Programs*. Springfield, IL: State of Illinois.

Kennedy, M. (2006). Seat Work. *American School and University* 78 (6): 24-29.

McDaniel, C. (1998). Budget-Minded Renovation Lights Up Students' Learning. *School Planning & Management* 37 (4): 38+.

McNicholas, T. (2006). Libraries and Media Centers. *School Planning & Management* 45 (3): 48-49.

Meeks, G. (2006). CAT6 Cabling? – Not! *School Planning and Management* 45 (1): 11.

Millard, E. (2006). The Perfect Plan. *District Administration* 42 (3): 60-64+.

NASSP. (1998). *The High School Magazine*: Facility Design and Management Issue 5 (5).

Scargall, H. (1999). Color: An Unsuspected Influence. *Library Talk* 12 (5): 11-12.

Smallwood, C. (1998). A Moving Checklist for Do-It-Yourselfers. *Book Report* 16 (4): 12-13.

Smartschan, G. F. (2006). The Design of Instructional Space. *School Planning and Management* 45 (1): 22-23.

Stevenson, K. & Pollier L. (1996). School Facilities Planning: At the Crossroads of Change. *School Business Affairs*: June, 9-13.

Weiss, S. (1997). Publish a Library Brochure. *The Book Report* 15 (4): 25.

Woolls, B. (1992). Where Have All the Balconies Gone? *School Library Journal* 38 (3): 182.

Library Facilities-Related Web Sites

American Library Association's Library Building Consultant's List
<https://cs.ala.org/lbcl/>

American Association of School Administrators: facilities related articles and news items
<http://www.aasa.org>

Baker & Berry Library Design Projects at Dartmouth
<http://www.dartmouth.edu/~library/BerryBaker/task.html>

Design Share Project for Innovative Schools
<http://www.designshare.com>

Doug Johnson's List of Facilities Questions
<http://www.doug-johnson.com/articles.html>

Ergonomics in the Library Media Center
<http://falcon.jmu.edu/~ramseyil/ergonomics.htm>

ERIC: Education Resources Information Center
<http://www.eric.ed.gov/>

Harvard Library Disaster Planning Site
<http://preserve.harvard.edu/emergencies/recovery.html>

The Ideal Library
<http://librarywalls.net/>

The Lighting Center
<http://www.thelightingcenter.com/ledalite/edu-comp.htm>

Maine School Library Facilities Handbook
<http://www.maslibraries.org/about/facilities/handbook.html>

Massachusetts Library Media Facilities Guidelines
<http://www.mslma.org/MediaForum/Apr2003/Facilities.html>

Missouri Association of School Librarians' Library Facilities Standards
<http://tiger.coe.missouri.edu/~masl/standard97/standard97.html#FACILITIES>

National Clearinghouse for Educational Facilities
<http://www.edfacilities.org/>

School Libraries.org Facilities Information
<http://www.school-library.org/csimpson_html/facilities.htm>

School Library Media Specialist: Facilities Planning

Glossary

ACM: asbestos containing material. Any materials containing asbestos have to be removed through special handling prior to renovation projects.

Add/Delete Pricing: the articulated cost to reduce or increase a given item such as data outlets. The add/delete price establishes a set price to add more outlets anywhere in the project or delete the same. Add/Delete pricing helps to keep down change order costs.

Alternate: work that is not part of the main project but may be added depending upon the final cost of the project. Bidders are required to bid each alternate as a separate item. Less than 50 percent of alternates end up being including in the final project.

American Institute of Architects (AIA): the professional association of American Architects.

Americans with Disabilities Act (ADA): federal legislation that addresses the needs of accessibility and accommodation for those with disabilities. Principally, ADA requires all new school facilities to be handicap accessible.

As Built Drawings: the final set of drawings provided to the school or district at the end of the project. These drawings should include all change orders and any other modifications made to the original construction documents.

Award: the formal acceptance of a bid or negotiated proposal. The award is normally made by the board of education.

Backbone: refers to the core cabling of the data network between wiring closets, the main distribution frame (MDF), and intermediate distribution frames (IDFs).

Bandwidth: refers to the carrying capacity of a communications network or segment. Bandwidth is generally expressed in units of kilohertz (kHz) or megahertz (mHz).

Bid Forms: forms used to provide a uniform method of comparing bids. Bids may be thrown out if the bidders do not meet the literal requirements of the bid forms.

Bid Notice: a legal notice posted in a newspaper or in other methods outlined by state law and school code. A bid notice often must be placed two or more weeks prior to the bid opening.

Bid Opening: the exact time and place when the school district staff will open the sealed bids. Bid openings are usually public meetings and most contractors will send a representative to the opening.

Bubble Diagram: a diagram used in the planning stages to depict space needs, traffic patterns, and relative locations of areas.

Built Ins: furniture or bookshelves that are constructed as part of the construction project and intended to be permanent. Wall shelving and some circulation desks would be examples.

Cable Tray/Ladder: a rack, generally parallel to the floor, which supports wires or cables. Cable trays are a more expensive option than using supportive rings in the ceiling.

Ceiling Plenum: also known simply as a plenum; the area between the ceiling and the underside of a structure that allows for cables to move without the need of wire mold.

Using a drop ceiling generally creates plenums. Cable used in plenums may need to be "plenum rated" to meet local fire codes.

Change Order: work that is different from that in the construction contract. Poorly planned projects tend to generate lots of change orders. These tend to add cost to the project.

Chases: small connecting spaces between floors that allow wires or pipes access to other floors or rooms.

Clerk of the Works: another title of the project manager. The title is particularly common is cases where the school district serves as its own general contractor.

Conduit: a flexible metal or plastic pipe that carries wire or fiber bundles throughout a building.

Construction Documents: the blueprints and related manuals and instructions created by the architects for the bidders to use in developing their bids. Many times, the bidders are charged for the documents to reduce the cost to the school district for creating them.

Contingency: a budget line or amount set aside in the bid process to cover any unforeseen costs or change orders that arise. This is sometimes referred to as an owner's contingency.

Design/Build: a type of project where the architect or contractor agrees to design the project as well as construct it. Such projects tend to save some time as construction documents are not necessarily completed prior to the start of construction. Design/Build projects are sometimes more expensive than projects bid in the traditional manner.

EAN: enterprise area network. A network in size between a local area network (LAN) and a wide area network (WAN) or a multi-building network that does not make use of wider area network delivery systems.

Educational Specifications: are the pedagogical requirements for the space. For a given project, they may be set out as a preamble to the bid specifications or given as a charge to the design team. How many students must be accommodated? What type of students are to be housed? Are there any special needs that must be accommodated?

Fiber: a strand of glass used for networking. Fiber comes in two basic types, single mode and multimode. Current network backbones sometimes require single mode with gigaspeed networks. Most previous data networking protocols used multimode fiber. It is important to ensure that one specifies the correct type or types of fiber for the project.

Final Completion: refers to when the punch list is completed and the entire project is done. The general contractor receives a final payment at this point.

Fire Stopping: a material, normally a putty-like substance, used to seal up holes in walls or other barriers through which wiring is run. Fire stopping prevents the spread of smoke and fire through the pathway used by the wiring.

General Contractor: the person or firm that oversees the entire project. A construction manager or a project manager on site often represents the general contractor. Occasionally, the school district will serve as its own general contractor.

Horizontal Cabling: cable running from the main distribution frame (MDF) or intermediate distribution frames (IDFs) to individual computers, printers, or wireless hubs. This cabling tends to be UTP (unshielded twisted pairs) otherwise known as copper.

HVAC: dealing with or relating to heating, ventilation or air conditioning. It is almost never referred to in any way but by the initials HVAC.

Indoor Air Quality (IAQ): the ability of an HVAC system to provide clean safe air within a building. IAQ can become a concern in remodeling projects when air-handling equipment is not completely modified to support the new physical spaces constructed.

Intermediate Distribution Frame (Facility) (IDF): a subordinate wiring closet within a building or campus. It is connected to the main distribution frame (MDF) by a back-bone also known as vertical cabling (usually fiber).

Isometric Drawing: shows the front, top, and right side views artificially rotated to 30° angles. This allows for more of a three dimensional view than traditional blueprints or floor plans.

LAN: Local Area Network: generally considered the network of a single building or complex.

Load Bearing Wall: a wall supporting part of the larger structure. Such walls can generally not be removed without significant expense and reengineering. In some cases, it may not be possible to remove such walls or columns.

Low-Voltage Wiring: a term for telephone and data cabling.

Main Distribution Frame (Facility) (MDF): the primary location of a school's data or telephone network(s). The wide area network (WAN) or Internet connections connect to the school's local area network (LAN) at the MDF. Also known as a wiring closet. Connected to intermediate distribution frames (IDFs) via vertical cabling also known as the network backbone.

Medium-Voltage Wiring: the general electrical wiring carrying power to normal class-room and office outlets.

Owner: in school construction projects, the school district or school board. You will often hear the contractors or architect refer to the owner.

Performance Contract: set up to guarantee the school or district a savings over time greater than or equal to the cost of the initial project. These projects often deal with energy efficiency issues such as replacing older light ballasts with more efficient lighting technology.

Pre-Award Letter: generated by the school administration to identify a bidder as the probable awardee of a bid. The pre-award letter is often generated if the board meeting where the bid will be formally awarded is several weeks away and the bidder is anxious to begin ordering materials.

Pre-Qualification: requires that bidders pass some level of screening in order to bid on a project. Those who would still bid without being pre-qualified could be rejected as non-conforming bids.

Programming Document: a questionnaire completed by the owner (school or district) to articulate the needs of staff within the space to be designed or renovated.

Project Management: normally a fee charged as a percentage of the total budget for the architect, engineer, or other to supervise the general contractor and ensure the plans are being followed exactly.

Punch List: used to list all of the items that need to be completed between substantial completion and final completion of the project. This list is generally created during a final walk through.

Raceway: any channel or tray used for holding or managing cabling. Some furniture now comes with built in raceways for cable management.

Reflected Lighting Diagram: effectively a floor plan of the ceiling showing the location of lights and other ceiling fixtures.

Scale: dimensions used to express relative proportion of drawings to the final project.

Sub-contractor: works under the direction of the general contractor. Sub-contractors usually focus on a single trade (skill). For instance, a general contractor may commonly use different sub-contractors for masonry, electrical work, and painting.

Substantial Completion: when the building or project is completed to the point where the staff and students can occupy the building. All work not yet completed should be minor and is articulated on a punch list.

Surge Protector: a part of the electrical system that stops unexpected electrical pulses from damaging electrical equipment such as computers and printers.

Trades (Building Trades): skilled trades people would include carpenters, electricians, masons, and painters. Often, architects will refer to workers as trades or tradesmen.

Turn Key Project (Turn Key Solution): the construction project will include furniture, computers, and other features. All the school or district will have to do is "turn the key" and open the door. In theory, the space will be ready for business. Turn key projects tend to cost more than ordering the furniture, computers, and other equipment as separate projects. Ease of administrating such a project may balance the additional costs.

Unit Pricing: the cost of an individual item. For instance, a bid for 30 video projectors may ask for a unit price if the bidder decides to purchase additional projectors depending upon the final amount of the successful bid.

UPS (Uninterruptible Power System or Supply): a system that provides power to computers or network electronics during a power outage. It is usually designed to allow the staff time to shut down the equipment during a longer outage so the equipment is not damaged.

UTP: Unshielded Twisted Pair: the most common type of network wiring consisting of copper wire and sheathing. It comes in a variety of types including category 5 (CAT-5) and gigaspeed.

Value Engineering: the method of deleting requested features, items, or areas until the project is within the scope of the budget. Value engineering is primarily done prior to bidding, but also may be done after bids are accepted to reduce costs.

Vertical Cabling: the network backbone or cable between the wiring closets, the main distribution frame (MDF), and the intermediate distribution frames (IDFs). Today, the backbone normally consists of fiber.

Voice Over IP (VoIP or VOIP): a telephone system that uses the data network for connectivity instead of being a separate system of telephone cables.

Walk Through: a tour of the building project. Pre-bid walk throughs take all prospective contractors on a tour of the area to be remodeled. A final walk through may create the punch list.

WAN: wide area network: generally considered a network comprising at least two locations not collocated. The five schools in a district would generally be connected by a WAN.

Wireless: generally refers to data networking without the use of cabling between the desktop computer and a wireless access point (hub). Wireless networks still require some wired infrastructure to support them. A building with a wireless network will still need a main distribution frame (MDF) and possibly one or more intermediate distribution frames (IDFs). The wireless network still will have a "wired" backbone.

Appendix A:
Questions to Be Answered During Site Visits

The answers to the following questions will help to gauge how similar the site's programs are to those planned for the new facilities:

- ☐ 1. What is the total student population? _____
- ☐ 2. How many staff members? _____
- ☐ 3. How is the library media center staffed?
- ☐ 4. What are the library media center's hours?

_____

- ☐ 5. How many classes can use the library media center at a time?_____
- ☐ 6. What is the average class size?_____
- ☐ 7. What are the largest class sizes?_____
- ☐ 8. How do teachers sign up to use the library media center?

_____

_____

- ☐ 9. What subject areas use the library the most?

_____

_____

- ☐ 10. What is the size of the collection (print, non-print, periodical holdings)?

_____

_____

- ☐ 11. What is the annual collection budget? _____
       Other budgets?
- ☐ 12. How do students use the library media center outside of class time?

_____

_____

- ☐ 13. What other programs or functions use the library media center space?

_____

_____

- ☐ 14. Does each member of library staff have their own work area or do
       staff rotate among several work stations or desks?

_____

_____

The answers to the following questions will help in determining the advantages and disadvantages of specific facilities:

☐ 15. Do you have good fields of vision and supervision throughout the media center?_____

☐ 16. How is the student flow facilitated through the media center?

_____

☐ 17. What accommodations have been made for the ADA?

_____

☐ 18. How do you control entrances and exits?

_____

☐ 19. How successful are your exit controls working?

_____

☐ 20. Do you have enough access to computers, the Internet, microforms?

_____

☐ 21. What are your thoughts about how student seating is arranged?

_____

_____

☐ 22. Where are your closed stacks? Who goes to retrieve those materials?

_____

☐ 23. Is there "off the floor" office space for the library staff?_____

☐ 24. What kind of curriculum related displays do you provide?

_____

☐ 25. Where do you showcase new materials? _____

☐ 26. How is the noise level when the media center is full? _____

☐ 27. How is the lighting in the media center? How could the lighting be improved?

_____

☐ 28. Is it easy to control the temperature in all areas? Why or why not?

_____

☐ 29. What area(s) do you use for direct instruction? What would you like to change about this area?

_____

_____

☐ 30. Do you use laptops and wireless networking in the library media center? If so, what issues should we consider in our planning?

_____

☐ 31. What provisions have been made for network infrastructure (MDF/IDFs)? How many servers do you have? Where are they located?

_____

_____

Furniture is another important area to address during site visits:

☐ 32. Would you use this same type of furniture if you were renovating the media center again?

_____

☐ 33. Are there times when you have to move or stack the furniture for other programs? How does that work for you?

_____

☐ 34. How does the computer furniture address cable management?

_____

☐ 35. How do you use the furniture to identify class areas or channel student use?

_____

☐ 36. Is the staff furniture acceptable?

_____

☐ 37. If you have "soft seating" in the library, what do you like/dislike about it?

_____

☐ 38. What are the dimensions of shelving, the circulation desk, and other workstations?

_____

☐ 39. What functions are difficult due to the way the circulation desk is designed?

_____

☐ 40. How does the furniture seem to be wearing?

_____

☐ 41. What problems have come up?

_____

Appendix B:
Library Media Center Programming Document

Questions to be answered by the planning team and other stakeholders for the library media center

Program questions:

☐ 1. What do you anticipate the student population will be when the center opens? In 10 years?

_____

☐ 2. How many students should the library media center accommodate at one time? _____

☐ 3. How many classes should the center accommodate at any one time?

☐ 4. How should the library media center be staffed?
Library media specialist(s) _____
Clerical staff _____

☐ 5. What should the library media center's hours be?
Should the library media center be open after school? _____
At night? _____
On weekends? _____
During the summer? _____
Why for each? _____

☐ 6. How do classes use the library media center? If you are on a fixed schedule, what type of resources do you need for those classes?

_____

☐ 7. How do you foresee students using the library media center outside of class time?

_____

☐ 8. How will teachers use the library media center?

_____

☐ 9. How will support staff use the library media center?

_____

☐ 10. How will parents use the library media center?

_____

☐ 11. What after school or evening activities will be held in the library media center?

_____

☐ 12. What size of a print collection would you expect?
     Non-print: videos, DVDs _____
     CDs _____
     Other _____

☐ 13. Should the library store class sets of textbooks? Of novels?
     Manipulatives?

     _____

☐ 14. What other materials should be stored or accessible through the library?

     _____

Student Control and Access:

☐ 1. In what ways will students come to the library media center?
     Individually from classes, from study halls or lunch, in small groups, in
     entire classes? Before or after school?

     _____

     _____

     _____

☐ 2. How should they enter?

     _____

☐ 3. How should they leave?

     _____

☐ 4. How will exits be controlled or secured?

     _____

☐ 5. What materials should they have open access to?

     _____

☐ 6. What materials should they not have open access to?

     _____

☐ 7. What materials should be teacher only?

     _____

☐ 8. Who will be primarily responsible for student supervision?

     _____

☐ 9. Where will that person have a separate workspace?

     _____

☐ 10. What areas must they be able to supervise at once?

     _____

☐ 11. What areas will not need supervision?

_____

☐ 12. How many students normally will be working together on a project?
     Will these students need a conference space?

_____

☐ 13. How many students will be working alone? _____
☐ 14. How many students will be selecting books? _____
☐ 15. How many computers will students need access to? _____
     For OPAC? _____
     For research? _____
     For productivity? _____
☐ 16. What will be the students' need to access multimedia and production
     software? Copiers?

_____

☐ 17. Should students have access to a restroom within the library media
     center? *(Consider extended hours needs here, when the rest of the
     building may be locked)*

_____

☐ 18. Should students have access to a drinking fountain within the library
     media center? *(Consider extended hours needs here, when the rest of
     the building may be locked)*

_____

Instruction:

☐ 1. Will there be direct large group instruction?
☐ 2. Will there be small group instruction?
☐ 3. Will teachers use the space for non-research instruction?
☐ 4. How will spaces be reserved?

_____

_____

☐ 5. Will reserve items need to be stored?
     On shelves or carts?
☐ 6. Will classes need both computer and table space at the same time?

_____

_____

Furniture:

☐ 1. How many student tables will you need? Why?

_____

☐ 2. What kinds of edges should the tables have? Why?

_____

☐ 3. Would you prefer laminate tops or wood?_____

☐ 4. Should the chairs be stackable? Why?

_____

☐ 5. Should the chairs be fabric, wood, or a combination? Why?

_____

☐ 6. Should task chairs be provided for the computers? Why?

_____

☐ 7. Should stools be used for the OPAC terminals? Why?

_____

☐ 8. Should any of the computers be at standing height? Why?

_____

☐ 9. Is any existing furniture going to be reused? If yes, which pieces and why?

_____

Library Workroom and Office:

☐ 1. Will each staff member need separate office areas?_____

☐ 2. Will the director need a separate office?_____

☐ 3. How many desks will be needed for the staff?_____
How many drawers in each desk? _____
What kind?

☐ 4. Should all the furniture be locking? _____
Should drawers all be keyed alike? _____

☐ 5. Where will money be stored?

☐ 6. Will side chairs be necessary at each desk? How many? _____

☐ 7. How many file cabinets will be necessary?
Locking: _____
Non-locking: _____

☐ 8. How many telephones?
Where? _____
Fax machine? _____

☐ 9. Will a worktable be needed?_____
How large? _____
How many chairs?_____

☐ 10. Will a conference table be necessary? _____
How many chairs? _____

☐ 11. Will additional processing space be necessary? _____

☐ 12. Should all storage be in cabinets or on open shelves? _____

☐ 13. What kind of stores will be kept in cabinets? _____
Locking?_____

☐ 14. What kind of stores should be kept on shelves?

☐ 15. Will any bins be necessary? _____

☐ 16. How many book carts will be stored? _____

☐ 17. Other equipment?

_____

☐ 18. Will volunteers need space for coats, purses, other items? _____

☐ 19. Will a sink with running water be necessary? _____

☐ 20. Should a restroom be included for the staff within the workroom? _____

☐ 21. Will there need to be a public restroom for after school hours? _____

Circulation/Service Desk:

☐ 1. What functions will take place here?

_____

☐ 2. What items need to be stored here?
Reference materials? _____
Office supplies? _____
Other? _____

☐ 3. What kind of computer needs does the circulation system have?

_____

☐ 4. Will books be returned here?

_____

- [ ] 5. Will anyone have a desk here?

_____

- [ ] 6. Will this space also be the reference desk? _____
- [ ] 7. Will there be any student workers? _____
- [ ] 8. Will there be a phone? For whom to use?

_____

- [ ] 9. Will there be a catalog terminal? For whom to use?

_____

- [ ] 10. Will students or teachers check out their own materials? _____
- [ ] 11. How high should the transaction counter be? _____

AV Equipment:

- [ ] 1. What equipment will be used in this area?

    Copy machines, _____

    laminator, _____

    other? _____

    By whom? _____

- [ ] 2. How many AV carts/How much equipment will be stored during the school year?

    During the summer?

- [ ] 3. Will laptop carts be stored in this area? If yes, how many?

_____

- [ ] 4. What will need to be plugged in?
- [ ] 5. What kind of repairs will be done on site?
- [ ] 6. Should all storage be in cabinets or on open shelves? _____
- [ ] 7. What kind of stores will be kept in cabinets? Locking?
- [ ] 8. What kind of stores should be kept on shelves?

_____

- [ ] 9. Will any bins be necessary? _____
- [ ] 10. What kind of lighting will be necessary in this area?

_____

_____

Noise Levels:

- [ ] 1. What is an acceptable noise level?
- [ ] 2. Should individual classes be separated acoustically?_____
- [ ] 3. Will computer or AV equipment affect the noise level?_____

Flooring:

- [ ] 1. Would you prefer carpet or tile? Why?

  _____

- [ ] 2. Will anyone be entering directly from the outside?_____

ADA Requirements:

- [ ] 1. Obtain a set of Americans with Disabilities Act (ADA) guidelines from the architect and designer.
- [ ] 2. Aisles, entrances, seating, and shelving will all be affected.

Display Areas:

- [ ] 1. What kind of materials do you want to display?

  _____

- [ ] 2. Where in the library should items be displayed?

  _____

- [ ] 3. Should students be able to access displayed items?_____

Other:

- [ ] 1. Should the public address system be heard in the library?_____
- [ ] 2. Where should fire extinguishers be located?

  _____

- [ ] 3. Where should fire or tornado evacuation plans be displayed?

  _____

- [ ] 4. Should the library be on a separate key from the rest of the school?_____
- [ ] 5. Should computer areas be separately keyed?_____
- [ ] 6. Will a security system be needed?_____
- [ ] 7. Do you need a pencil sharpener?_____

Appendix C:
Sample Specifications Form for an Area
of the Library Media Center

AREA:
Normal Student Capacity: _____ Maximum Student Capacity: _____
Desired Volume Capacity: _____ Print: _____ Non-Print:
General Description: (attached floor plan of present space if applicable)
Activities to be Conducted:
Furniture Needs: _____ Tables _____ Chairs _____ Desks _____ Other

Storage Needs:
     Open _____
     Closed_____
     Secure_____

Collocation Needs:

Number of Data Outlets:_____

Number of Electrical Outlets:_____

Special Considerations:

Appendix D:
Computer Lab Programming Document

Questions to be answered by the planning team and other stakeholders for computer labs

Program Questions:

☐ 1. How should the computer lab be staffed?
_____
_____

☐ 2. What do you anticipate the student population will be when the school opens? _____

In 10 years? _____

☐ 3. How many students should the computer lab hold?

☐ 4. What should the computer lab hours be?
Should the computer lab be open after school?
At night? _____
On weekends? _____
During the summer? _____
Why for each? _____

☐ 5. How will classes use the computer lab?
_____
_____

☐ 6. Will classes regularly meet in this lab or sign up for time as needed?
_____
_____

☐ 7. How do you foresee students using the computer lab outside of class time?
_____
_____

☐ 8. How will teachers use the computer lab?
_____

☐ 9. How will support staff use the computer lab?
_____

☐ 10. How will parents use the computer lab?
_____

Student Control and Access:

☐ 1. In what ways will students come to the computer lab?

_____

☐ 2. How should they enter?

_____

☐ 3. How should they leave?

_____

☐ 4. How should exits be controlled or secured?

_____

☐ 5. What materials should be teacher only?

_____

☐ 6. Who will be primarily responsible for student supervision?

_____

☐ 7. What areas must they be able to supervise at once?

_____

☐ 8. What areas will not need supervision?

_____

☐ 9. How many students will normally be working together on a project? Will these students need a conference space?

_____

_____

☐ 10. How many students will be working alone?

_____

Instruction:

☐ 1. Will there be direct large group instruction?_____

☐ 2. Will there be small group instruction?_____

☐ 3. Will students be working as groups of two? _____

   Of four? _____

   Larger groups?_____

☐ 4. How should spaces be reserved?

_____

☐ 5. Will classes need both computer and table space at the same time?_____

Computer Equipment:

☐ 1. How many computers will students need access to?_____

☐ 2. How should the limit on the number of students using the lab be determined?

_____

☐ 3. What size monitors do you anticipate using?_____

☐ 4. Do you prefer desktop computers, mini-towers, or towers? Why?

_____

☐ 5. Will the computers need USB ports? _____

Firewire ports? _____

Floppy drives? _____

Zip drives? _____

CD-ROM drives? _____

☐ 6. What type of network connections will you need?

_____

☐ 7. What other devices will you need?

Scanner, _____

DVD drive, _____

audio mixer? _____

Other? _____

☐ 8. How many printers will you need?

Laser? _____

Color? _____

Plotters? _____

Other? _____

Where should they be located?_____

Do any of the printers need to be controlled by an adult? _____

☐ 9. Will there be a server for the lab?_____

☐ 10. Where should it be located?

☐ 11. How will it be secured? Who should have access to it?

_____

☐ 12. Does any other network equipment need to be secured?

Switches? _____

Routers? _____

Other? _____

Presentation Equipment:

☐ 1. What kind of projection devices will be used?
Video projector? _____
LCD? _____
Overhead? _____

☐ 2. How should these items be mounted?
_____

☐ 3. From where should they be controlled? Does the system need a wireless mouse or keyboard?
_____

☐ 4. Will a switcher be required to control input from multiple sources?_____

Furniture:

☐ 1. How many computer workstations will you need?_____

☐ 2. What will the average "station" include?
CPU, _____
keyboard, _____
writing space, _____
Other? _____

☐ 3. Will any storage space be necessary for each student?_____

☐ 4. Would you prefer keyboard trays or not? Why?
_____

☐ 5. What type of chairs would you prefer?
Leg or sled base? _____
Wheels or no wheels? _____
Upholstered, wood, or plastic? _____
Arms or no arms? _____

☐ 6. Will you need regular (non-computer) tables? Why? How many?
_____

☐ 7. What kinds of edges should the tables have? Why?
_____

☐ 8. Would you prefer laminate tops or wood?

☐ 9. Should any of the computers be at standing height? Why?
_____

☐ 10. What kind of furniture should be used for printer stands? Scanning stations?

_____

☐ 11. Is any existing furniture going to be reused? If so, which items and why?

_____

Teacher and Lab Supervisor Space:

☐ 1. How many desks will be needed for the staff? _____

☐ 2. How many drawers in each desk? What kind?

☐ 3. Should all the furniture be locking? Should drawers all be keyed alike?

_____

☐ 4. Will side chairs be necessary for the desk? _____

☐ 5. How many file cabinets will be necessary? _____
Should they be legal or regular? _____
Locking: _____
Non-locking: _____

☐ 6. Will the desk need a computer and printer? Any other equipment?

_____

☐ 7. Will a telephone be necessary? Where?
A speaker phone? _____
Fax machine? _____

☐ 8. Will a conference table be necessary?
How many chairs? _____
Could a peninsula or bullet shaped desk serve the same purpose? _____

☐ 9. Should all storage be in cabinets or on open shelves?

_____

☐ 10. Where will software be stored?

_____

☐ 11. Where will manuals be stored? How many?

_____

☐ 12. Will any textbooks be stored? _____

☐ 13. Will any student disks, CDs, or USB drives be stored? _____

☐ 14. Will computer carts be used at all? _____

☐ 15. Will computer carts need to be secured in the lab from other areas?_____

☐ 16. Will "spare equipment" be included in the lab? _____

☐ 17. What kind of lighting will be necessary in this area?

_____

Flooring:

☐ 1. Would you prefer carpet or tile? Why?

_____

☐ 2. Will anyone be entering directly from the outside? _____

ADA Requirements:

☐ 1. Obtain a set of Americans with Disabilities Act (ADA) guidelines from the architect and designer.

☐ 2. Aisles, entrances, and seating will all be affected.

Display Areas:

☐ 1. What kind of materials do you want to display?

_____

☐ 2. Will instruction sheets or pathfinders need to be available for student use?

_____

☐ 3. Should students be able to access displayed items? _____

Other:

☐ 1. Should the public address system be heard in the computer lab?_____

☐ 2. Where should fire extinguishers be located?

_____

☐ 3. Where should fire or tornado evacuation routes be displayed?

_____

☐ 4. Where should the clock be located?

☐ 5. Should the computer lab be on a separate key from the rest of the school? _____

☐ 6. Should server or software storage areas be separately keyed?_____

☐ 7. Will a security system be needed? _____

☐ 8. Do you need a pencil sharpener? _____

Questions Relating to Network Closets

☐ 1. What equipment will be included within this closet?

Switches? _____

Routers? _____

Servers? _____

UPS? _____

Telephone equipment? _____

☐ 2. Will the equipment be mounted into equipment racks?

Wall mounted? _____

Or will furniture be required? _____

☐ 3. How far will this closet be from the main closet (MDF) or from other IDFs? _____

☐ 4. What areas will this closet serve?

☐ 5. Is this closet in an area of the building that will possibly see further expansion? How would that expansion affect the needs of the network or wiring closet?

_____

_____

☐ 6. What kind of ventilation will be necessary for this space?

_____

☐ 7. What will the electrical needs be for this closet?

☐ 8. How should this area be lighted?

☐ 9. Should a phone be included in this closet? _____

☐ 10. How should this area be keyed?

☐ 11. Will any non-network or phone equipment be stored in the closet? How might that affect the network equipment?

_____

☐ 12. Will manuals, disaster recovery plans, or other printer materials be stored here? _____

☐ 13. Should a desk or table be included within the closet? _____

☐ 14. Will any spares be kept in here? What kind?

_____

Appendix E:

Issues to Be Addressed in Bid Specifications

General Qualifications about the Bidder:

- [ ] 1. Name and location of business.
- [ ] 2. Experience in this type of work.
- [ ] 3. Experience in a school setting.
- [ ] 4. Years in business under this name.
  Under a previous name.
- [ ] 5. Licenses held by the business.
- [ ] 6. Certifications held.
- [ ] 7. Association memberships.
- [ ] 8. Trade references.
- [ ] 9. Business references.
- [ ] 10. School references.
- [ ] 11. Financial statements.

Working Conditions:

- [ ] 1. Working hours.
- [ ] 2. Prevailing wages, if applicable.
- [ ] 3. Safety precautions.
- [ ] 4. Insurance.
- [ ] 5. Performance bonds.
- [ ] 6. Access to specific areas of the building.
- [ ] 7. Access to keys, phones, fax machines.
- [ ] 8. Change orders. Who may recommend and approve.
- [ ] 9. Clean up. Daily and at project completion.
- [ ] 10. Storage of equipment and product. Staging areas.
- [ ] 11. Delivery times.
- [ ] 12. Right to remove workers.

Schedules and Coordination:

- [ ] 1. Schedule of work completion and progress payments.
- [ ] 2. Pre-construction meeting.
- [ ] 3. Weekly progress meetings.

- [ ] 4. Date of substantial completion (when you can use the space).
- [ ] 5. Partial use and right of occupancy.
- [ ] 6. Tests and inspections.
- [ ] 7. Date of final completion.
- [ ] 8. Pre-bid meeting.
- [ ] 9. Pre-bid inspection.
- [ ] 10. Identification of project manager.
- [ ] 11. Final submittal of project documentation.
       Shop drawings.
       As built CAD drawings.
- [ ] 12. Liquidated damages.
- [ ] 13. Bonus for early completion.

Other:

- [ ] 1. Submission of sample product.
- [ ] 2. Ability to substitute like items.
- [ ] 3. Warranties.
- [ ] 4. Hazardous materials.
- [ ] 5. Disposal of refuse or old equipment.
- [ ] 6. Repairs and patching.
- [ ] 7. Firestopping.

Each Section of the Bid Specifications Should Include:

- [ ] 1. Summary,
- [ ] 2. References,
- [ ] 3. Specifications,
- [ ] 4. Quality assurance and submittals,
- [ ] 5. Recommended or required suppliers, and
- [ ] 6. Specific or unique conditions.

Schedule of Values:

Delineate costs in a schedule of values so comparison of bids is simple and costs cannot be hidden in other areas of the bid. Fixed values should be required for uniform additions or deletions from the general bid. An owners' contingency fund may be included. Any shift work costs should be borne in the base bid as well.

Appendix F:
Sample Schedule of Values for Computer Equipment

	Value
30 Desktop Computers:	
Processor: Intel Pentium 4.0 GHz processor	
Memory: 2 GB 533Mhz SDRAM (must allow for expansion to 4GB)	
Monitor: 17-inch color monitor (16 inch viewable image) .28 dot pitch	
Graphics accelerator: Integrated 4MB graphics accelerator	
Hard drive not less than 80 GB hard drive	
Floppy drive: 3.5 inch 1.44MB internal floppy	
USB Ports: Front access USB port	
CD-ROM: 20x min internal CD-ROM drive	
Sound card: 32 bit audio with output to speakers	
Case: locking desktop (all locks to be keyed the same)	
Keyboard: 104+ keyboard	
Mouse: two-button MS mouse with mousepad	
Operating Systems: MS Windows XP on CD-ROM	
Network Card: 3Com PCI 10/100/1GB TP Ethernet	
Warranty: three-year warranty on site	
Total computer cost including delivery:	
Cost to install and connect to the network:	
Cost per additional computer:	
Credit per deleted computer:	
2 Printers:	
Network ready black and white laser printer	
Allows 8 1/2" x 11" and 8 1/2" x 14" paper sizes	
Speed no less than 32 sheets per minute	
One year on site warranty	
Total printer cost including delivery:	
Cost to install and connect to the network:	
32 Patch cables:	
Category 5 (UTP) Ethernet patch cables, 6 feet long	
Total cable cost:	
TOTAL:	

Appendix G:
Common Table & Workstation Sizes and Shapes

Squares & Rectangles

24x24 30x24 36x24 42x24 48x24 60x24 72x24

30x30 36x30 42x30 48x30 60x30 72x30

36x42 36x48 36x60 36x72

42x42 42x60 48x48 48x60 48x72

Round Tables

36 42 48

Conference Half Circles

48x24 60x30

Bullet Shaped Conference Table

Radius Edge Table

36x48 36x60 36x72
36x48 36x96

Common Corner Shapes

 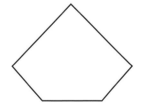

Index

A

Acoustics and noise reduction, 50, 62
Administrative support, 10
Americans with Disabilities Act, 32, 106,
    112,120, 128
Architect, 2,6-10, 17, 19, 23, 47, 50, 92, 97
Archives 47
Audiovisual 14, 18, 19, 64, 100, 119
        Production area, 41-43
        Storage area 50, 100

B

Bids
Documents, 9, 54, 64, 94
RFPs, 93, 98
Specification, 50, 56, 58, 92-98, 102
Break room (staff lounge), 6
BISCI, 18

C

Chairs, 36, 51-53, 117-118, 126-127
Circulation (service) desk, 16, 25, 32, 37-40,
    46, 113
Collection size, 28, 29, 32, 64
Color, 30, 36, 52, 54, 61-64, 98
Community Access4, 21-22, 26
Computer
        Areas, 44, 45, 88, 120
        Furniture, 16, 52, 54, 79, 96, 113
        Labs, 11, 20, 23, 43, 65, 79, 123
        Laptops, 3, 16, 32, 77-78, 113
        Mobile labs, 77-78
        OPACs, 45, 116-117
        Repair areas, 3, 42, 43, 119
        Specifications, 59, 79, 93
Conference areas, 2, 40-41, 50, 87, 116
Council of Educational Facilities Planners, 8, 19

D

Displays, 16, 26, 112
Display shelving 32-33

H

HVAC systems, 43, 50, 108

L

Lab supervisors, 70, 76, 123
Language labs, 81
LAN/WAN, 45,46, 58, 77, 108
Library media center
        Entrance, 17, 17, 25, 61, 64, 112
Lighting, 17, 60, 61

M

Media distribution system, 14, 42, 44
Microforms, 16, 26, 30-31, 40, 62, 112
Moving, 99-101
Networking, 2, 4, 9, 16, 23, 43, 56-58, 77
        Closets, 43-44, 46, 58, 78, 129

O

Office space, 16, 46, 56, 112

P

Politics, 6, 9
Project Team
        Composition, 5, 6
        Leadership,6 8

S

Seating 112, 120, 128
        Soft, 16, 36
        Student, 16, 34, 36, 57
Security, 3, 4, 25, 42, 61
        Materials, 26, 40, 76, 120, 128
Shelving, 2, 8, 25, 100
        Analysis, 2, 8, 27, 28, 30, 31, 113
        Closed, 33
        Compact, 33
        Display, 32
        Equipment, 42, 47
Signage, 33, 63-64
Site visitations, 15-16, 97, 102
Story area, 41, 48, 64
Structural load (floor), 33, 51

T

Tables, 32, 35-36, 117, 126
Telephones, 42, 118, 130
Time lines, 96-98

V

Video projectors, 60, 66, 76, 78

W

Wireless networks, 2, 3, 16, 57, 58, 77
Wiring,
        Data, 2, 42, 54, 56, 59, 96
        Electrical, 4, 9, 42, 56-59, 129
        Types of, 56-58
Wiring Closets, 43-44, 46, 58, 78, 129
Workrooms, 26, 46-47, 50, 118